Bread and butter, toast and jam, scones and clotted cream—baked goods have a long tradition of being paired with spreads to make their flavors and textures sing. As a baker with a passion for plants, Sarah Owens, author of the James Beard award–winning *Sourdough,* takes these simple pairings in fresh new directions. Spread some **Strawberry & Meyer Lemon Preserves** on a piece of **Buckwheat Milk Bread** for a special springtime treat. Top a slice of **Pain de Mie** with **Watermelon Jelly** for a bright taste of summer. Lather some **Gingered Sweet Potato Butter** on a piece of **Spiced Carrot Levain** for a warming fall breakfast. Make a batch of **Dipping Chips** to serve with **Preserved Lemon and Fava Bean Hummus** for an inspired snack. Wow brunch guests with a spread of **Sourdough Whole-Grain Bagels, Lemony Herb Chèvre,** and **Beet-Cured Gravlax.** The recipes here offer a thoroughly fresh sensibility for the comfort found in a simple slice of toast spread with jam.

TOAST & JAM

TOAST & JAM

MODERN RECIPES FOR RUSTIC BAKED GOODS
AND SWEET & SAVORY SPREADS

Sarah Owens

Photographs by Ngoc Minh Ngo

ROOST BOOKS
BOULDER
2017

Contents

Recipes

Introduction

A Manifesto of Crumbs

THIS BOOK IS A GENTLE CHALLENGE, enabling you to bring better food choices into your life with intention. Whether you are attracted to scratch cooking out of choice or because your arm was twisted by a health crisis, the following recipes are pantry staples that will easily improve your quality of living through enhanced flavor and the convenience of knowing what you put into your body. The result is an opportunity to relish in the bounty of the seasons with a kitchen free from unnecessary additives. If you are inspired to empower yourself with a few simple techniques, baking and cooking with whole foods becomes both a joy in the tactile process and a surprisingly satisfying end result with delicious reward.

Modern society has traded the promise of efficiency and thrift for highly processed food-like products. We have bartered for convenience and subsidized commodities in lieu of health, happiness, and community. It is no surprise that we are suffering as a whole because of it. The real cost of cheap food is our quality of life, emerging in chronic conditions such as digestive disorders and depression that are on the rise at unprecedented rates.

Many have backlashed, spawning fears of gluten and restrictive diets, providing the promise of strength and health in the face of our own demise. A feeling of helplessness in the shadow of corporate influence has led us down the narrow road of demonizing what we don't understand. It is true of our food choices and now, frighteningly, our politics. The foundation of our lives, however, need not be drawn from the trepidation of a dubious food industry and a shallow comprehension of its systems.

We have the power to do something bold and daring: We can bake a loaf of bread or make a pot of jam. Being involved in what we eat is an opportunity to engage creativity with the better aspects of contemporary culture. Every ingredient will have an intended purpose and known identity.

It is an opportunity to relish in leisure that nourishes the body and the spirit. It is an opportunity to say "I choose" and celebrate life.

Scratch cooking is reclaiming what we are all entitled to, taking back not only nutrition but also flavor from the institutional forces that dominate modern food production. Let's strip it all down and see what happens, shedding the unpronounceable ingredients wrapped in plastic packaging that crowds our bins.

Plunge your hands instead into a bowl of cool water, fragrant stone-ground flour, and a smidgen of sea salt. Watch as the magic unfolds and this seemingly inert mixture comes alive. Feel the weight of a golden loaf as you embrace its warmth from the oven. Breathe deeply the seasonal aromas plucked from flowering trees that make your house feel like a home. Relish in the effort of massaging vegetables, coaxing them to release juices for their own preservation. You have just enabled a transformative revelation and transcended the fluorescent aisles of the supermarket. Congratulations, you have begun a new and delicious journey toward self-sufficiency.

There was a time when pooling resources and gathering around the hearth were standard practices. We were well fed, sharing the bounty of our harvests and breaking bread by firelight. Indeed, many still practice this in lieu of choice for anything different. In contrast, the modern aspects of the privileged world have fast-forwarded to a culture eager to advance through technology at an environmental and spiritual cost. Considering this anemic hyper-lapse, I beg you to slow your step and examine the fundamentals. Embrace the simplicity of very humble ingredients that, when nurtured by your own hands and the gift of time, become a tremendous revelation. It is not so much a nostalgic throwback but true advancement from having our diets orchestrated by others.

Instead of mourning the detachment from our food and its preparation, choosing independence from processed foods has strangely become a flag of the gentrified, a status symbol of wealth. Quality ingredients certainly don't come cheap, and this manifesto is by no means another attempt at food shaming. If you struggle to stock your pantry with high-cost organic, stone-ground flour, start with the best quality ingredients you can afford. If the drought-driven prices of market tomatoes or berries send your breathing into hyperventilation mode, consider nursing a plant on your fire escape or taking a walk through the woods to pick a pint.

At best, a gorgeous loaf of crusty hearth bread will emerge with a jewel-colored jar of preserved fruit waiting at breakfast. At worst? You may end up with a doorstopper or chicken feed. The tradeoff is experience and practice. Go ahead and accept that it takes a minute to nail down the techniques of baking bread and preserving your own food. Beating ourselves up over not producing an Instagram-worthy dish right out of the gate should be the least of our worries. Employing the methods used in this book—especially those that pre-digest our food through methods of lacto-fermentation—sends us on a journey toward healing from the preoccupation of the materialistic, image-driven world.

If it looks a little wonky at first, know that you are at least feeding yourself real food rather than fluff.

Whatever your motivation, cook or bake with ingredients of integrity and feel your body respond. Take joy in the smile you put on someone else's face because what they are eating is genuine and made with intention. Not sure where to start? Have a conversation with a farmer and ask him or her what they're excited about harvesting that season. Take some of what inspires them home and preserve it in a jar. Visit a market that specializes in foods of specific ethnic communities and try to understand the value and histories of those traditions. Taking the time to consciously source ingredients, preserving the toils of an unassuming farmer, or seeking context for our food are all humble but bold steps forward to restoring a proper quality of life. It is a beautiful and poetic gesture, providing a meditative practice for the individual and delicious and satisfying nourishment for the friends and family who share in the process. When we encourage that which is simple to thrive with abundance, little else is needed in life.

Naturally Leavened

A Primer on Baking

WHEN YOU CHOOSE TO BAKE a loaf of naturally leavened bread, you are combining a few rather basic and inert ingredients with powerful forces of nature to create a biochemical set of reactions. Stone-ground flour plus water plus microbes plus salt plus time and temperature is a formula that allows fermentation to commence and flavor compounds as well as gases to be released as by-products. Those carbon dioxide gases become trapped in a web of dough that has been made strong and stretchy by kneading both during mixing and often afterward. These trapped gases leaven the dough and give it rise, eventually signaling cues that reveal when it is ready to be subjected to high heat in a steamy environment. Bubbles swell at the surface, acetic and lactic acids build, improving the aroma and souring the flavor of the dough. The result is an easily digestible loaf made possible by the power of microbes coaxed into breaking down the otherwise troublesome components of grain, namely gluten and phytic acid compounds. When you slice into your first loaf of bread, its creamy crumb and caramelized-crust aroma may very well distract you from these persuasive benefits.

This process is a transformation that is supernatural in every sense and has the power to enchant and bring us closer to and in participation with the fundamental laws of the universe: fire, water, earth, and air. Perhaps it is not so much magic as it is alchemy, converting basic matter into an elixir for prolonged life. If we welcome and nurture the process, it becomes a type of divine transcendence that hypnotically inspires us with visceral as well as spiritual satisfaction.

A Simple Sourdough Starter

In my book *Sourdough* I detailed how to begin a sourdough starter culture using a yeast water method whose vigor I find encouraging to many beginning bakers. However, all you really need to get a culture bubbling is some quality flour and pure water to farm the microbes responsible for fermentation. Set it in a warm spot (70°F to 75°F is ideal), and in about 1 week, you will have a responsive culture that is ready to leaven bread.

---

210 g / 1¾ cups freshly milled stone-ground all-purpose flour

210 g / ¾ cup plus 4 tablespoons filtered water

In a small bowl, stir together 60 g / ½ cup flour and 60 g / 6 tablespoons water to form a thick and sticky mixture with no dry lumps remaining. Cover loosely with cheesecloth or a clean towel and set in a warm location for 2 to 3 days or until you detect a light, boozy scent and see bubbles breaking the surface. Discard half and add another 60 g / ½ cup flour and 60 g / 6 tablespoons water and stir to combine. Replace the cheesecloth and allow to ferment at room temperature for 8 to 12 hours. The mixture should be bubbly and active after this time.

Discard half of the mixture and add another 90 g / ¾ cup flour and 90 g / ½ cup plus 1 tablespoon of water. Allow to ferment again for 8 to 12 hours. Once it is fragrant with a creamy, yeasted scent, perform the float test by dropping a dollop of the starter into a cup of water. If it floats, the wild yeast is active enough to produce carbon dioxide gases as a by-product of fermentation. If it sinks, perform one or two more feedings or extend the feeding time before trying again.

Once your new culture passes the test, feed it daily with equal parts flour and water to the weight of the starter. (For example 90 g starter + 90 g water + 90 g flour = a 1:1:1 ratio.) This will produce a starter that is 100% hydration for the recipes in this book. Feed it daily if kept at room temperature, or store it in the refrigerator and feed it weekly, always discarding (or using!) some, but not all, of the original starter before each feeding. I like to keep at least 2 heaping tablespoons of starter (about 50 to 60 g) on hand at all times.

Store your starter in a jar with a loose-fitting lid to prevent it from drying out. Mason jars with a flip top lid are excellent, as the rubber gasket can be removed, allowing the lid to be fully closed but still loose.

KITCHEN NOTE Getting a sourdough culture started is a slower process in the winter than in the warmer months. If after a week you do not see (or smell) bubbling fermentation activity, place a heating pad turned to the lowest setting underneath your jar, or place the jar in the oven with the light on (just don't forget about it!), or in any other spot in your house that is warmer than the ambient temperature of your kitchen.

BREAD BAKING BASICS

"I arise in the morning torn between a desire to improve (or save) the world and a desire to enjoy (or savor) the world. This makes it hard to plan the day."

—E. B. WHITE, quoted in the *New York Times*, July 1969

The recipes presented in this book use natural leavening (sourdough), quick leavening (baking powder and soda), and conventional leavening (baker's yeast) as Agents of Deliciousness fighting the Evils of Bland Uniformity. When baking bread, each recipe has different requirements and techniques to make it successful depending on the type of leavening, flour, and hydration, and the temperature of your kitchen. I suggest you read through the instructions and list of ingredients before planning your bake; you need not have prior experience with bread to achieve tasty results. As with any discipline, however, ample practice, determined effort, and the gift of time will move your technique from a technical skill to an artful craft.

The following is a quick-reference guide of alphabetical terms integral to performing the bread-baking recipes in this book.

ESSENTIAL EQUIPMENT

Baker's Couche: A type of baker's linen that can be used to shape dough during final proofing, giving support to the loaves as well as preventing them from sticking together. This is particularly helpful when making A Modest Baguette (page 53) and Moonbread (page 50).

Banneton: A round or oblong basket used to shape and support dough in the final stages of bread proofing. Also called a brotform or proofing basket. If you are using a Dutch oven to bake your loaves, make sure the shape of the banneton fits within the diameter of the Dutch oven.

Bench Knife or Dough Scraper: Ideal for lifting bread dough and pastries from your work surface, this helpful tool will also assist in shaping wet dough in recipes such as A Modest Baguette (page 53) or Moonbread (page 50).

Dutch Oven: These versatile baking pots are constructed of heavy, heat-retaining materials such as cast iron or enamel-coated cast iron, allowing you to balance the heat and humidity needed to produce quality loaves in your own home kitchen. When used properly, they produce a hearty and rustic loaf with a thick, crispy crust and moist interior crumb. Please see individual recipes for complete instructions.

Hearthstone: A heavy slab made from ceramic, stone, or steel to retain heat, increasing the overall performance of your home oven in the production of hearth-style breads. It is useful in baking free-form breads such as Lavash (page 80) or other breads that do not fit inside a Dutch oven, such as A Modest Baguette (page 53) or ciabatta-shaped Moonbread (page 50). A hearthstone must be used in combination with steam in order to achieve a thick and crusty loaf. Please see individual recipes for complete instructions.

Lame: A double-sided blade used to score bread, often attached to the end of a handle. If making your own, use a thin, flexible blade and attach it to the end of a Popsicle stick, chopstick, or whittled-down branch.

Loaf Pans: Two types of loaf pans are used in this book: most often a 9-inch standard tin, but sometimes a 9 × 4-inch Pullman tin. For either, choose a heavy gauge, preferably of aluminized steel made with a corrugated bottom.

Scale: If you are serious about becoming a home baker and fermentationist (and if you bought this book, I assume you are!), please do purchase an inexpensive scale that measures in grams. The recipes in this book include volume, common market measurements, and weight measurements in grams that are often rounded up or down a few grams for ease of use. Bread recipes and vegetable ferments in particular are formulated by weight, with the percentages of ingredients calculated according to their biochemical interactions.

Although cultivating intuition in response to climatic and ingredient variables is key, using an accurate scale helps to eliminate guesswork in measuring by volume and ensures that your time invested yields more successful results. All ingredients, including liquids, are measured in grams to prevent you from having to switch display screens mid-mix.

Thermometer: An instant-read thermometer removes the guesswork from gauging water temperature in dough mixing. An oven thermometer is also incredibly helpful for determining appropriate bake times, as every oven (particularly electric) has a different behavior.

BASIC TECHNIQUES AND BREAD VOCABULARY

Autolyze: A resting period in the initial stages of dough mixing, during which the flour is allowed time to hydrate and gluten proteins assemble to build dough strength.

Bench Rest: A resting period used most often after pre-shaping dough. This allows the dough to relax before being shaped into its final, tighter form.

Bulk Proof/Ferment: The period after mixing and working the dough either through kneading or a series of slap-and-folds. During this time, yeast consume the sugars present in the flour and release a by-product of carbon dioxide gas that leavens the dough. If using a sourdough culture, bacterial fermentation also occurs, releasing flavor compounds referred to as acetic and lactic acids. This is most often done at room temperature, but it may be performed in a colder, refrigerated environment as well.

Crumb: The interior of a loaf, defined by the holes or alveolation in the bread. A well-developed crumb is judged not necessarily by the size of the holes but rather by their consistency in relation to one another, indicating fermentation was thorough and shaping was done correctly. Depending on the type of flour used and its relative hydration, crumb performance will vary dramatically. For example, the Buttermilk Rye (page 39) is a style of bread that will never have a large and open crumb due to the ingredients, fermentation schedule, and hydration level. It is valued for its density, unlike Moonbread (page 50), which has a moderate to open crumb structure reminiscent of honeycomb.

Crust: The exterior of the loaf where sugars concentrate and caramelize to produce a light golden to deep and dark brown toothsome outer layer. Generally hearth-style loaves are baked *bien cuit*, or "well done," to achieve a thick and bold, dark crust. Other doughs such as enriched Oat Flour Brioche (page 65), Pain de Mie (page 67), or Buckwheat Milk Bread (page 61) use butter and eggs to tenderize the loaf and are baked to have a thin, more delicate skin. Both methods should produce rich flavor compounds, though they are quite different in character.

Kneading: Working the dough by hand to gain strength and elasticity. Done most often with doughs that are moderately hydrated to develop the gluten structure necessary to trap the gases that leaven bread.

Mixing Dough: Mixing dough by hand brings together all the wet ingredients, including leavening, with all the dry ingredients to initiate dough fermentation. The leavening is often simply a 100% hydration sourdough starter (equal parts flour and water by weight) that has been refreshed 8 to 12 hours previously or a customized leaven according to the recipe that includes specific flours. Commercial yeast may also be used. These leavening agents work with additional flour and a source of hydration—often water but sometimes juice, dairy, or eggs and also sweeteners that are mixed well until no dry lumps remain. When making 1 to 2 loaves it helps to work in a rhythmic squeezing motion, rotating the bowl with one hand while mixing with the other. Be sensitive to the textural feeling and temperature of the dough as you work, as this will help you to gauge fermentation during the succeeding steps.

Poke Test: Using a floured finger, gently push into the surface of the dough. If the indentation springs back, it needs more time to proof before baking. If the indentation lingers, it is ready to bake.

Refresh: Often referred to as a "feed" when maintaining a sourdough starter. For the purposes of this book, starter is fed with equal parts flour and water by weight. This is done at room temperature 8 to 12 hours before the intended use, allowing it time to become active and visibly bubbly.

Retard: Slowing fermentation by cooling the dough in the refrigerator at temperatures ideally held between 38°F and 41°F. This improves the flavor as well as the digestibility of the grain.

Scoring: Cutting into the surface of a loaf before loading it into the oven to be baked. This is done most often with a straight or curved razor blade or with a special baker's tool called a lame. Scoring is performed so that the loaf may expand in a controlled fashion, releasing steam in the process. To adequately score a loaf, all you need is one slash performed with an even motion halfway to three quarters from the edge of the loaf to a ¼-inch depth. Once you get the hang of it, however, you may want to play with more decorative patterns, adding shallow cuts for visual appeal.

▶ Mixing dough

Shaping: The handling of dough to form it into a particular arrangement for baking. This is typically done before the final proofing and involves two steps: pre-shaping with a short bench rest and a final shaping that pulls the dough into a tighter, more coercive form.

Specialized shaping procedures are described in the recipe instructions themselves, but the following are instructions to create a basic boule shape used for the Dutch oven method in this book: Remove the dough from the bowl and divide it on a floured work surface. Fold the edges of the dough ball into the center to create a circular shape, using your bench knife to assist with wet dough. Place the dough seam-side down on the work surface, cover it with plastic wrap or a damp towel, and allow it to relax and bench rest for 10 to 20 minutes before final shaping. To final shape, repeat the pre-shaping process with greater coercion of the dough to create surface tension. Do not tear, rip, or overfondle the dough, as this will lead to a heavy, dense bread. With naturally leavened dough, it is important to create surface tension in the loaf to trap the gases in final proofing without deflating the dough in the process. If you are used to making bread with commercial yeast, do not punch down bread leavened solely with sourdough before shaping. This final step is a delicate balance that requires intuitive practice, using the dough's fermentation activity to guide your movements.

▲ Shaping dough

▲ Slap-and-fold

Slap-and-Fold: A way to work and develop wet dough shortly after mixing, in lieu of kneading. This encourages further strength in the dough that can trap leavening gases and will result in a more aerated, open crumb once baked. To perform the slap-and-fold technique, remove the dough from the bowl and slap it against a clean work surface, dragging the dough to stretch it before folding it over itself. This step is repeated in a rhythmic fashion until the dough transforms from a shaggy mass into a more cohesive, smooth form, about 5 to 7 minutes. If the dough begins to tear on the surface, cover it with plastic wrap or a damp towel and allow it to rest for a few minutes before returning to the movement.

Stretch-and-Fold: A way to work wet dough in its mixing bowl in lieu of kneading on the work surface. Reach to the bottom of the bowl and gently pull a handful of the dough up and over itself, folding it to the center. Rotate the bowl with a series of turns until all of the dough has been stretched.

BREAD STORAGE

One of the questions I get asked most is how to maintain the freshness of bread for the longest amount of time. Loaves leavened with sourdough will naturally resist mold and have a longer shelf life due to powerful antifungal compounds produced during the fermentation process (unlike breads that are only leavened with conventional yeast). There are however, several considerations to keep in mind when storing bread of any kind.

Bread goes stale due to moisture loss, and it is important to understand this process before choosing your preferred storage method. As soon as bread has cooled from the oven, the starches go through a chemical crystallization called starch retrogradation whereby moisture is expelled. Loaves can also lose moisture by simply being exposed to air.

To properly store bread, allow the loaf to completely cool before wrapping it in a natural, breathable material such as heavy paper or beeswax wrap. Plastic can be used, but it may trap moisture and prevent the loaves from "breathing," increasing the potential for mold and decreasing the crispness of the crust over time.

Bread, especially sourdough, is best stored at room temperature for up to one week. If you must store it for longer, consider freezing it or, as a last resort, keeping it in the refrigerator. It is important to note that the refrigerator will cause the bread to dry out faster but will inhibit mold growth due to cooler temperatures.

Bread freezes incredibly well, halting starch retrogradation at low temperatures. So don't hesitate to do batch baking when you have the time! Allow the bread to cool completely, wrap it in paper, and then completely seal it in plastic, excluding as much air as possible. It will keep in the freezer for up to two months. You may preslice the bread and defrost the slices directly in the toaster as needed. If thawing a whole loaf, place it in the refrigerator to allow the crumb to reabsorb the melting ice crystals slowly and prevent any sogginess that might occur at room temperature.

A Celebration of Nature's Abundance

A Primer on Preserving

THIS BOOK IS AN ODE TO THE SEASONS, to stockpiling the bounty and relishing in the clockwork of cultivating and harvesting flavor at its peak. When we nourish ourselves with what responds to daylight and temperature, our bodies align with our environment and receive optimal benefits, especially during the warmer months. There is little comparable to eating a tree-ripened peach warmed by the sun or a blackberry plucked straight from the brambles. But what of the dormant season? Are we to be satisfied with root vegetables, nuts, and grains until the sun warms our faces once again? By mastering just a few clever methods, we can save the sensations of summer for the leaner times ahead. Not only do we gain in choice and quality in our pantry, but we can also preserve beautiful food traditions that have been passed down for generations through various cultures and heritages. A well-stocked pantry is a reflection of both honoring what nature provides and investing in the future.

Living in a dense, urban area such as New York provides a very different experience in preservation than my mother and grandmothers experienced in their days of canning apples and freezing tomatoes. My family includes generations of preservationists who grew most of what was put up for the winter. I will never forget the smell of the damp, earthen basement when I was sent to retrieve a jar of jam for Sunday morning biscuits on the farm. A whole year's worth of hard work was stacked up and waiting for the shorter days of winter. After harvesting from the garden, the women of my family toiled over the hot stove during the warmest months of summer to make sure we didn't have to run to town when the roads iced over. Thankfully, in our modern day of information sharing, we may now choose a number of different methods to employ when our kitchens are pregnant with seasonal produce. Although traditional recipes made with large amounts of sugar are standard preserving practice for fruit, alternatives, such as low-sugar pectin, work equally as well, albeit with slightly different texture.

If you are lucky enough to be overwhelmed by the bounty of your garden, CSA share, local farmers' market, your neighbor's cow, or the great abundance of nature, it is time to start thinking about preservation. As the title implies, there is a strong emphasis in this book on jams and fruit preserves, but I have included many other recipes that may enhance the use of baked goods, as life is made sweeter by so much more than sugar. Some of these recipes require more time and equipment than others, but there are simple ways to ensure that you can have the flavors of summer when snow is falling outside your door. Some of the methods outlined ahead rely on natural fermentation to not only preserve but also enhance nutrition and amplify flavor. Other techniques use large amounts of salt or sugar as microbial inhibitors and to achieve a particular set in jams, jellies, and marmalades. These are meant to be eaten in moderation and considered a delightful, occasional splurge. Jams that are made with small amounts of additional sugars have a softer, almost slippery set and are to be frozen or eaten within a short time after preparation. These are indicated as such in the recipes themselves.

Other items we don't always consider as seasonal can be preserved with a little care. Grass-fed cow's milk always tastes sweeter in the spring, making it the perfect time to attempt Crème Fraîche (page 208). If you have access to pastured milk or are just simply looking to be more self-sufficient and cost saving, cultured dairy recipes are fairly simple and incredibly rewarding accompaniments for toast as well as jam. Pacific wild-caught king or sockeye salmon is available for only a few weeks in mid- to late summer, making the Beet-Cured Gravlax (page 213) a wonderful reason to splurge on a large fillet.

All of these methods are based on traditional techniques that have been handed down for generations either in my own family or through cultures I find inspiring. Some are examples of culinary staples from where I grew up in the South, while others hail from exotic lands I have visited in my travels. All of these are markers of food history that speak volumes about origins and identity, about family and what we hold dear. My hope is that you not only learn the science and methods behind these recipes but are also inspired to incorporate them into your own seasonal traditions, adjusting them to your own needs and taste preferences within the boundaries of food safety.

CANNING BASICS

There are a few rules to keep in mind when preserving food in jars, and the following instructions are based on USDA guidelines for heat processing or canning food for long-term storage.

Home canning ensures that you have access to natural foods year-round without crowding your refrigerator or freezer. All you need is some basic equipment and a little time to perform a heat processing step after your jams, jellies, or pickles are prepared. This type of processing works with foods that are acidic enough (a pH of 4.6 or lower) to inhibit the growth of botulism and have enough sugar to inhibit the growth of mold. Properly canned foods will keep in a cool, dry place for up to one year.

EQUIPMENT

Most kitchens are already equipped with the items necessary for heat-processing, but you will need to purchase glass canning jars with rust-free, two-piece metal lids. The recipes included in this book are for small-batch canning and require little more than a deep stock pot and a jar lifter (or salad tongs in a pinch). The pot should be large enough to immerse the jars completely in water by at least one inch, with ample room for the water to boil. A rack that fits into the bottom of the pot is a true asset, as this protects the filled jars from direct heat. In addition, canning funnels and magnetic lid wands can help with maneuvering the jars and lids in and out of the water bath. A kit with these tools can be purchased inexpensively and will streamline your production if you anticipate canning throughout the season. (Please see the appendix on page 238 for resource suggestions.)

A heavy, deep, and wide preserving pot will contribute to the successful set of jams, jellies, and preserves. Not only will a heavy-bottomed pot conduct heat efficiently without the risk of scorching the bottom, but it also exposes a large surface area to air, which aids in the evaporation and thickening of your mixture.

Finally, although a sieve, large spoon, and bowl will suffice, a food mill will make processing many fruits easier, yielding a consistent and pleasing texture to preserves such as Caramel Apple Bourbon Butter (page 129), Gingered Guava and Chili Preserves (page 140), and Tamarind Rum Jam (page 144).

STERILIZING JARS

Place the required amount of clean jars on a rack in a large stock pot or boiling water canner. I often include at least one extra jar, as fruits and vegetables vary in volume and weight depending on the season, sometimes blessing you with a little extra. If you have a fancy jar that isn't appropriate for long-term storage but is heatproof and beautiful for presentation, consider sterilizing it as well for immediate enjoyment or refrigeration/freezer storage.

▲ Sterilizing jars

Cover the jars with water, position the lid, and bring the water to a simmer over medium heat, being careful not to let it boil. For ease of handling, place the lids (but not the screw rings) in a small saucepan, cover them with water, and heat until just under boiling. Sterilize the jars and lids for 10 minutes before turning off the heat. Leave the hot water–filled pot on the stove eye for later use in heat processing the filled jars.

▲ Skimming foam

▲ The set test

SKIMMING FOAM

Many fruits become viscous as you boil them into jam, trapping air as they cook, which results in a frothy foam. While there is nothing terribly wrong with this foam, it has an unpleasant mouthfeel and a compromised keeping quality in the finished product. To avoid accumulating excessive amounts, simply skim and discard the foam with a spoon as the jam cooks.

THE SET TEST

It is not always clear when homemade jams, jellies, and preserves are ready to transfer into sterilized jars. Over time you will begin to notice the more subtle cues, but this simple test is an easy way to determine whether the mixture will set well upon cooling.

KITCHEN NOTE Depending on the fruit, whether it is fresh or previously frozen, the recipe, and the type of pectin you are using (if any), your jam, jelly, or preserve may take longer than others to firm up and set after processing. If the sealed jars have completely cooled and the mixture is still runny, try placing the jars in the refrigerator, as this rapid cooling will often encourage a better set. Once they have firmed up, remove the jams from the refrigerator and allow them to come to room temperature once again. If they return to a liquid state, you can reprocess your jam, altering the ingredients to get a better set. Otherwise, simply keep them stored in the refrigerator until ready to consume.

Place a clean, thin glass or ceramic plate in the freezer at least 10 minutes before you are ready to test your jam. When you are near the end of the suggested cooking time, remove the jam from the heat and place a small dollop onto the cold plate. Return the plate to the freezer for 2 to 3 minutes. Test for a set by nudging your fingertip into the dollop of jam. If a wrinkled skin has formed or your finger mark remains, your jam has reached a setting point and is ready to be ladled into jars. If the jam pools into a runny liquid, this is an indication that it is not ready and needs more cooking time or an adjustment of sugar, acid, and/or pectin.

HEAT-PROCESSING FOR LONG TERM STORAGE

When your jam, jelly, or pickle is ready to process, remove one jar at a time from the hot water bath, draining any residual water back into the pot. Place the jars on a clean sheet pan for ease of cleanup. Do not dry the jars with a towel; the extra water will evaporate from the heat. Ladle or pour the hot preserve or pickle into the hot jar, leaving about one-quarter inch of space from the top, and slide a clean spatula or knife down the inside of the jar to release any trapped air. Top off the contents if necessary and repeat until the jars are filled. Carefully wipe the rims with a clean, damp towel and position the hot lids before firmly screwing on the rings.

Place the filled jars back into the hot water bath, making sure they are covered by at least one inch of water, then position the lid on the pot and bring the water to a full boil over high heat. Process for 10 minutes, starting a timer when the water reaches a full boil. When the timer rings, turn off the heat, remove the lid from the pot, and allow the steam to clear for about 5 minutes. Remove the jars from the water bath without tilting them, and place them upright on a towel to let them cool undisturbed.

After about 24 hours, check the lids for a seal by pressing down on the center of each one—they should show no movement. Lids that pop with movement when pressed have not sealed properly and must be refrigerated immediately. Label the sealed jars and store them in a cool, dry location, ideally between 50°F and 70°F.

TROUBLESHOOTING JAM

One of the most frequent problems that occurs when making jams, jellies, and preserves is a lack of set. Although I prefer a softer, almost silky set and often leave the pectin out altogether to make a syrup, you may wish to troubleshoot and seek a firm or stiff consistency. A lack of set can be due to any number of reasons, so before you reprocess the mixture, consider what might be the culprit:

Not enough sugar—Most of us have reservations about adding the amount of sugar that is often called for in most traditional jams. Because most recipes in this book hold back on the amount of sugar, if you did not use a low/no-sugar pectin, your fruit may not set. If reprocessing, try adding ¼ to ½ cup more sugar.

Not enough acid—Pectin needs the presence of acid in order to bond with sugar and fiber at a temperature of 220°F. Try adding 1 to 2 more tablespoons of lemon juice or white vinegar upon reprocessing.

Not enough pectin—Different fruits have varying amounts of pectin, depending on their composition and their ripeness upon harvest. Read the packet instructions carefully before using to make sure you are following the manufacturer's suggested amounts. If reprocessing, try adding an additional teaspoon or tablespoon of pectin, depending on the label's instructions.

Not enough fiber—Jellies that use only fruit juice or puréed fruit don't have much fiber and therefore often require more pectin than jams do. If your jelly does not set well, try increasing the amount of pectin according to the label's instructions.

Over/undercooking—Overcooking after adding pectin will break down its structure, decreasing the chances your jam will set. Alternatively, undercooking prevents the proper set of jams and jellies. After stirring pectin into the hot mixture, you should cook the preserves for only 1 to 3 minutes maximum before the jam reaches a setting point.

LACTO-FERMENTATION BASICS

Fermentation is a metabolic process in which yeast or bacteria convert sugars into both carbon dioxide and acidic flavor compounds. It is the magical process that preserves or enhances the flavor of our most cherished foods: It naturally leavens bread, transforms grain into whiskey, helps turn cocoa beans to chocolate, and produces olives. It has been used for thousands of years to provide mind-altering joy juice to the masses in the form of wine and also coffee. Many of these such ferments are produced mostly on a large, commercial scale, but armed with a simple understanding of microbes, a home cook can also harness the power of fermentation to preserve food. For the purposes of this book, I will refer to two types of fermentation: that of grain (sourdough or natural leavening, which was discussed on page 7) and vegetable pickling (or lacto-fermentation).

TEMPERATURE

For most types of fermentation mentioned in this book, a temperature range of 70°F to 75°F is preferable. Lower temperatures are fine but will result in slower fermentation, especially for pickles. Higher temperatures (80°F or more) will encourage your pickles to go soft or your bread to taste curdled and sour from overproofing.

SAFETY

Most fermentation methods culture lactic acid bacteria (*Lactobacilus sp.*) not only to increase the digestibility of grain and increase the probiotics of vegetables, but also to keep these foods safe. This incredible genus of microbes lowers the pH of foods, making them inhospitable to the "bad guys" that cause spoilage. For this reason, use jars made of nonreactive materials, such as glass or ceramic.

EQUIPMENT

If you are culturing pickles, you will need adequate air exchange. Keep in mind that the jar will need to accommodate your chosen method of weighting the vegetables underneath their brine, as well as the release of carbon dioxide as the pickles ferment. If you do not accommodate these two factors, you will end up with an explosive (and possibly even dangerous) mess.

One of the few rules of successful pickling is to keep the vegetables submerged in their brine while also allowing the opportunity for off-gasing. I fermented pickles safely and successfully for years without purchasing any specialized weighting equipment, simply using a plastic bag filled with water or a heavy plate or small jar that fits inside the container. If you like gadgetry and have space in your kitchen, refer to the Resources section (page 238) for a few alternative suggestions. These cleverly engineered crocks or jars will help to eliminate room for error and prevent mold from taking root on the surface of your ferments. You can also discourage this from happening by using a large leaf to cover the mixture before adequately weighting it. If a thin layer of mold appears, simply remove and discard this leaf layer.

Pantry Notes

T HIS BOOK WAS WRITTEN in three rather humble locations: one in proximity to my summer garden in Louisville, Kentucky; another on the road while doing ingredient research in Central and South America; and the last in a 200-square-foot beach bungalow in Queens, New York. In every situation, my intentional and chosen lifestyle is not one of superfluous amenities, although I do have a tendency to splurge while seeking quality ingredients. Upon choosing the recipes to include, I considered what most readers would be able to source with a little Internet savvy and minimal monetary investment. If you decide to commit to a lifetime of baking, canning, and fermenting, I do, however, suggest that you invest in some quality equipment that will endure over time and will ensure high performance. Please refer to the appendix in the back of this book for suggestions.

VEGETABLES AND FRUIT

When selecting fruits and vegetables for making jams, jellies, and preserves, choose only the best quality and those that are in season, if possible. To prevent spoilage, cut away any lesions or moldy areas before making preserves, especially for long-term storage. Those used within one to two days of harvest yield the best results, as they contain the highest amounts of vitamins and minerals as well as pectin content, which is important to getting a good set if you are making fruit preserves. If you have a glut of ripe fruit that you do not have time to process, consider pitting and coarsely chopping before placing in the freezer in Ziploc bags. Although this encourages the fruit to release its juices, altering the texture of the cooked preserve, it is a fine alternative to letting the fruit overripen before using. So go ahead and sign up for your local CSA, grow your own, or frequent a nearby farmers' market in high season when you can.

MAKE IT WILD

There are a few ingredients that are foraged from the wild, such as violets, dandelions, elderflowers, and sumac. Edibles that are found in their natural state without the complex selection and breeding of man have been found to be highly concentrated in nutritional benefits. Be careful to source from locations that are free from soil contaminants, and always leave some behind for the birds and the bees.

FLOUR, SEEDS, NUTS, AND SPICES

Working with fresh, organic, stone-ground flours will give your breads an unparalleled flavor profile, nutritional boost, and appearance. The process of stone grinding preserves all parts of the grain and produces flours and breads with stronger aromas and higher nutritional content than those made from commodity grains milled in large processing facilities. Commercially processed flour, including glutinous bread flour that gives dough its strength, is roller-milled to ensure that it is shelf-stable for up to one year. Although it has the advantage of long-term storage life, it does not include any of the precious germ oils that are responsible for the flavor and health benefits of whole grains. When purchasing stone-ground flour in bulk, seal it well in airtight containers or bags and store it in the freezer, bringing it to room temperature before mixing into dough.

If you have never baked with flour that is stone ground, especially from grains grown in your region, be prepared for a different performance in your chosen recipe. These types of flours have increased enzymatic and bioactivity, which speeds up the fermentation process and makes your dough literally feel and act more alive—be prepared and don't let your dough overproof, especially in summer! Also, depending on where they are sourced, different flours will need different levels of hydration. I will never forget working with one of my favorite all-purpose flours made from Sonoran wheat grown and milled in Arizona. As you can imagine coming from a high-desert environment, the flour was quite thirsty! Mixing dough by hand helps you judge these variables, adjusting water content accordingly: If the dough or batter feels incredibly stiff, add about a tablespoon of water or milk at a time until it feels workable. Likewise, some bread flours made from wheat grown in humid environments may have a weaker protein structure or require less water upon mixing. It is better to hold back the water, adding small amounts at a time, rather than adding flour later. When purchasing from a small-scale, local miller, chat with them first about their flours. This engagement helps you become a better baker and lets them know someone cares about the hard work they have invested in honing their craft!

As with all perishable pantry items, it is important to purchase seeds, nuts, and spices from sources that have frequent turnover to ensure that they are as fresh as possible. Store these items in a cool location in separate airtight containers. If you do not think you will use the nuts or seeds within a few weeks of purchase, store them sealed well, in the freezer (much as you would stone-ground flour) to ensure that their oils do not go rancid. Spices should be used within six months of purchase so they remain potent and flavorful.

SALT

Salt is used for a number of reasons in this book. It slows or regulates the fermentation of vegetables and also dough. It works well as a preserving agent in canning and gives pickles their characteristic flavor. Salt also draws out excess liquid from vegetables, fruits, and meats, firming their texture and balancing their flavor with other preserving agents such as sweeteners.

I prefer to keep fine sea salt on hand for all my baking, pickling, and fermenting needs, and flaked or kosher salt that is easily pinchable to use as a finishing flourish. When it comes to salt, density matters, and the different varieties available all have different weights for the same volume. (Please refer to the measurement index at the back of the book for examples.) Pickling salt is excellent for canning because of how easily and quickly it dissolves into the brine, but be aware that it is the finest you can choose—use a scale for accuracy if you are making substitutions. Avoid using table salt, as it contains anticaking agents that may leave a chemical aftertaste or interfere with the canning process. If you are using sea or earth salt for pickling or canning, try to use a variety that has no natural coloration, as this may cloud your end product.

BAKER'S YEAST

Baker's yeast is a commercially produced single strain of *Saccharomyces cerevisiae*, found in fresh cake and dried, granulated forms. It is used in home and commercial baking to speed the fermentation process of available sugars and appreciates a warm and humid environment to thrive. Active dry yeast is used in this book in combination with other fermentation methods such as sourdough or cultured dairy to produce a delicious and nutritious end result without compromising quality. Be mindful that the amounts required in each recipe may be cut in half in the warmest summer months to keep the dough in check. Store sealed containers of yeast in a cool location in your pantry away from heat and humidity.

PECTIN

Pectin is a naturally occurring polysaccharide present in the cell walls of plants, which, with the right balance of acidity, bonds with fibers and sugar at a temperature of 220°F. When this happens, a pleasing set or gelling occurs in jams, jellies, and many preserves. We can either harness the natural pectin in the fruit itself or add commercially produced pectin to induce gelling. Some fruits (like currants, blueberries, cranberries, apples, citrus, and certain grape varieties) contain much higher amounts of natural pectin. Counterintuitively, under-ripe fruits are much higher in pectin and are helpful in recipes that do not call for commercially added pectin.

Commercial pectins are often extracted from either citrus or apples in two different iterations: high-methoxyl pectin and low-methoxyl pectin. The high-methoxyl variety works well in the presence of large amounts of sugar and is used in most traditional jams and jellies. Low-methoxyl pectin works with low- or no-sugar jams but only in the presence of calcium. For this reason, it is incredibly important to read the label's instructions before following the recipes in this book. All the following recipes that require pectin use a low- or no-sugar pectin that already has calcium included. Be aware that some brands require the extra step of mixing a calcium water for the pectin to work.

KITCHEN NOTE It is possible to make your own pectin stock from the cores and peels of citrus or under-ripe green or crab apples. I find this useful only in jams with high amounts of sugar, such as Vanilla Marmalade (page 137) or Fennel, Pear, and Black Pepper Preserves (page 131). For an example of making apple stock, refer to Caramel Apple Bourbon Butter on page 129.

For tips on getting the right set (or what to do if your jam doesn't set!), flip to pages 22–23.

SUGAR

In most fruit preserves, we use a hefty dose of sugar for two reasons: to thicken the fruit and to help the finished product keep for longer. Sugar and acid work together at a temperature of 220°F to bond and set with pectin, which is either naturally present in the fruit or added in the form of a commercial product. When this happens, we get what is called a proper set, or thickening of the preserve. Sugar also works to inhibit the growth and reproduction of certain molds that decrease the shelf life of your product. Sugar does not inhibit the growth of the deadly *Clostridium botulinum*, commonly known as botulism and found everywhere in our environment. Although *C. botulinim* is never completely eliminated in heat processing, an acidity of 4.6 or lower on the pH scale will ensure that its bacterial spores do not proliferate to produce toxic levels in its preferred anaerobic environment that is the hallmark of canned foods. For this reason, it is important to add an acidifier such as lemon juice or vinegar to foods with a high, alkaline pH level.

Many of the recipes in this book are prepared with the lowest amounts of sugar necessary to encourage them to set, save for a few. Those that are not heat processed are best stored in the refrigerator or frozen until ready to use. If freezing your preserves, leave a good inch of headspace from the rim of the container to allow for expansion.

PART ONE

TOAST

1

Breads

"Perhaps this war will make it simpler for us to go back to some of the old ways we knew before we came over to this land and made the Big Money. Perhaps, even, we will remember how to make good bread again."

—M. F. K. FISHER, *How to Cook a Wolf*

BREAD IS SIMPLY a joy to nurture. With the gift of time and some diligent patience, this creative practice will fill you with curiosity and beg you to bake yet another loaf. This particular set of recipes was chosen for its ability to provide an appropriate canvas for a myriad of flavor accompaniments.

◄ *Top left to right*: Drop Biscuits, Lavash, Miche, Sourdough Rye Crackers. *Middle*: Spiced Carrot Levain, Seeded Tahini Pain Rustique. *Bottom left to right*: Black Bread, Seeded Tahini Pain Rustique, Buttermilk Rye.

Miche

— MAKES 1 LARGE LOAF —

This large round loaf has delicious flavor, especially if made with fresh, stone-ground wheat flour. It sports a somewhat tight crumb perfect for jam, without the density of a 100 percent whole wheat bread. I developed this formula while living in Kentucky, using locally grown and milled flour with a lower protein content and weaker gluten structure. Wheat grown in this region is considerably less elastic than that from colder, more arid climates, leading to a dough that often spreads and pools during shaping. This is due partly to the shortened winter dormancy, but also to the rains and humidity that often come before harvest. Repeatedly told that I couldn't make bread with flour from Kentucky, I put a beautiful high-extraction Turkey Red Wheat flour to the test and came up with this perfectly delicious loaf that rivals any others in flavor complexity and pleasing crumb. It harkens to the French tradition of the miche and is appropriately named for its low profile, large boule shape, and whole wheat flavor.

FOR THE SOURDOUGH LEAVEN

25 g / 1 tablespoon 100% hydration active
    sourdough starter, refreshed (page 10)
30 g / 3 tablespoons water (70°F)
45 g / ⅓ cup plus 1 tablespoon whole wheat flour

FOR THE DOUGH

430 g / 1¾ cups plus 3½ tablespoons water
    (70°F)
400 g / 3½ cups Type T-85 wheat flour
    (high-extraction bread flour)
110 g / heaping ¾ cup strong bread flour
40 g / heaping ⅓ cup whole rye flour
11 g / 2 teaspoons fine sea salt

BUILD THE SOURDOUGH LEAVEN

In a large bowl, stir together the starter and water to form a slurry. Add the flour and stir to combine; the leaven will be somewhat stiff. Cover with plastic and allow to ferment at room temperature until puffy and aromatic, 8 to 12 hours.

MIX THE DOUGH

Combine the water and flours in a medium bowl and mix until the flour is hydrated and no lumps remain. Cover with plastic and allow to autolyze at room temperature for 1 to 2 or up to 4 hours. Sprinkle the salt over the dough. Break the sourdough leaven into small pieces and add it to the dough. Mix with your hands until the leaven is completely incorporated and no visible streaks remain. Cover with plastic and allow to bulk ferment at room temperature for about 3 to 4 hours, stretching and folding in the bowl every 30 to 45 minutes.

SHAPE THE DOUGH

When the dough is puffy and increased in volume by about one-third, preshape it into a round boule. Cover with plastic and allow to bench rest for 10 to 30 minutes. Final shape according to your preference and banneton shape and place the dough seam-side up in the well-floured banneton. Cover with a towel and then plastic and refrigerate for 8 to 24 hours.

BAKE

Remove your loaf from the refrigerator and allow it to come to room temperature for about 1 hour or until it passes the poke test. Preheat a Dutch oven (preferably enamel coated) to 500°F on the middle rack of the oven for 20 minutes.

Sprinkle a touch of cornmeal onto a piece of parchment paper cut to fit the bottom of the Dutch oven and carefully flip your loaf onto it, seam-side down. Score the top of the loaf about ¼ to ½ inch deep with a razor blade or lame. Carefully lower the parchment paper and loaf into the preheated Dutch oven, position the lid, and return it to the oven. Reduce the oven temperature to 480°F and bake with the lid on for 20 minutes. Remove the lid and bake for another 12 to 20 minutes or until the crust is brown.

TRY IT WITH . . . This is an excellent all-around table loaf with unmatched versatility in flavor. It is perhaps my favorite bread to use in making **Baked Pain Perdu**, as it soaks in enough of the egg mixture to produce a toothsome but custardy result. This whole grain bread is delicious served simply with good cultured butter or cheese and most any seasonal jam, but it can also be used for making sandwiches or **Garlic Crostini** and is a fine choice for any cheese plate or charcuterie board.

> **KITCHEN NOTE** I prefer my bottom crust to be as thick and dark as possible, but if you are using a non-enameled cast-iron pot, you will need to tip the loaf out of the Dutch oven after about 25 minutes of baking time to prevent the bottom from burning before the loaf is done. This must be done carefully to avoid burning yourself. Finish baking directly on the middle rack for an additional 12 to 20 minutes.

Seeded Tahini Pain Rustique

— MAKES 2 TIN LOAVES OR 1 LARGE BOULE —

Sourdough has played an important role in my personal path to wellness, harnessing the powers of fermentation to make grains and seeds more digestible. Fortunately, it also makes them more flavorful. For this book I wanted to experiment, incorporating techniques that would quicken the baking process without sacrificing the benefits of sourdough fermentation. This recipe uses a large amount of liquid sourdough in the pre-fermentation stage and incorporates granulated baker's yeast into the final dough. A few tablespoons of tahini adds to the unmatched nutty flavor and soft crumb of this bread, making it an excellent sandwich loaf or rustic beauty of a boule. The result is a chewy crumb full of flavor and easy to digest, combined with a thick and crispy crust that keeps well. The process can be completed in anywhere from 12 to16 hours with limited hands-on time compared to most sourdough breads. Mix up the leaven on Friday night so you can have a warm loaf ready for weekend brunch. If you desire to use sourdough leavening only, simply follow the same fermentation schedule, placing the shaped loaves in the refrigerator and lengthening the final cold proofing time to 4 to 6 hours.

FOR THE SOURDOUGH LEAVEN

50 g / 2 tablespoons 100% hydration active
    sourdough starter, refreshed (page 10)
250 g / 1 cup plus 2½ tablespoons water (75°F)
220 g / 1½ cups plus 2 teaspoons bread flour
30 g / ¼ cup whole spelt flour

FOR THE SOAKER

15 g / 1½ tablespoons whole flax seeds
15 g / 1½ tablespoons chia or poppy seeds
15 g / 1½ tablespoons black or white sesame seeds
15 g / 1½ tablespoons amaranth or quinoa
15 g / 1½ tablespoons pepitas or sunflower seeds
60 g / 6 tablespoons water (75°F)

FOR THE DOUGH

80 g / ¼ cup plus 2 tablespoons water (100°F)
40 g / 2 heaping tablespoons Tahini Sauce
    (page 157)
150 g / 1 cup plus 2 teaspoons bread flour
½ teaspoon active dry yeast (optional)
80 g / ¾ cup whole spelt flour
25 g / ¼ cup whole rye flour
8 g / 1½ teaspoons fine sea salt

FOR THE OUTER COATING

60 g / about ½ cup mixed raw seeds such as
    those used in the dough

PREPARE THE LEAVEN AND SOAKER

To build the leaven, place the starter and water into a large bowl and stir to a slurry. Mix in the flours until well hydrated and no lumps remain. Cover and leave to ferment at room temperature until bubbly and aromatic, 8 to 12 hours.

To prepare the soaker, place the seeds in a separate small bowl and add the water. Cover and allow to rest at room temperature until you are ready to mix the dough.

MIX THE DOUGH

To the bowl with the leaven, add the water, tahini, flours, and yeast (if using), and mix with your hands until a shaggy, somewhat sticky dough forms with no dry lumps remaining. Cover and allow to autolyze at room temperature for 20 minutes. Sprinkle in the salt, mixing with your hands to evenly distribute.

Remove the dough from the bowl and perform the slap-and-fold method on a clean surface for about 5 minutes. When the dough feels consistent and springy, pat it out into a rectangle, about 1 to 1½ inches thick. Spread an even layer of the soaker mixture onto the surface of the dough. Fold the top and bottom thirds of dough to the middle and coat with more of the soaker. Continue in this fashion, rubbing the seeds evenly onto the new folds, until all of the soaker is used.

Clean and lightly oil your bowl and return the dough, tossing to coat. Cover and allow the dough to bulk proof for about 2 hours in a warm location, stretching and folding it at least once.

SHAPE THE DOUGH

Once the dough has doubled in size and feels springy and elastic but still tacky to the touch, remove it from the bowl onto a lightly floured surface. Preshape to a round boule, cover, and allow to relax for 10 minutes. Spread the seeds for the outer coating on a shallow plate and perform the final shaping. Roll the shaped loaf in the seeds and transfer the boule to a well-floured banneton, seam-side up. Cover and allow to finish proofing in a warm location for about 1 to 1½ hours, performing the poke test to check for readiness. Alternatively, or if it is a hot summer day, retard the shaped loaf in the refrigerator for up to 2 hours to slow fermentation and increase flavor.

If you desire to make tin loaves, divide the dough into two equal pieces and follow the shaping and baking directions for Pain de Mie on page 57. Roll the separate loaves in seeds to coat before placing them in the tins seam-side down, and continue proofing as directed above.

BAKE

Preheat a Dutch oven (preferably enamel coated) to 500°F on the middle rack of the oven for 20 minutes. Sprinkle a touch of cornmeal onto a piece of parchment paper cut to fit the bottom of the Dutch oven and carefully flip your loaf onto it, seam-side down. Score the top of the loaf about ¼ to ½ inch deep with a razor blade or lame. Carefully lower the parchment paper and loaf into the preheated Dutch oven, position the lid, and return it to the oven. Reduce the temperature to 480°F and bake with the lid on for 20 minutes. Remove the lid and bake for another 12 to 20 minutes or until the crust is brown.

TRY IT WITH . . . This is an excellent sandwich bread, especially when shaped into tin loaves. It has a deep, nutty aroma that can host a variety of spreads and flavors. It is my favorite bread for making any variation of avocado toast!

KITCHEN NOTE I prefer my bottom crust to be as thick and dark as possible, but if you are using a non-enameled cast-iron pot, you will need to tip the loaf out of the Dutch oven after about 25 minutes of baking time to prevent the bottom from burning before the loaf is done. This must be done carefully to avoid burning yourself. Finish baking directly on the middle rack for an additional 12 to 20 minutes.

Buttermilk Rye

— MAKES 2 MEDIUM LOAVES OR 1 LARGE DOOR STOPPER —

Rye is one of the most deliciously earthy flours you can use to make naturally leavened bread. This loaf is hearty in character and complex in robust flavor with a bright finish that pairs equally well with meats, strong cheeses, and bold fruits. Rye flour does, however, exhibit a wildly different performance in dough as compared to other flours, and if you are new to working with it, you may find yourself scratching your head with a sticky finger, wondering if you have somehow measured the wrong ingredients. Don't doubt yourself, as this is a wonderfully forgiving dough that can be coerced into a tin loaf or free-formed into a well-floured proofing basket. It benefits from a long and slow bake as well as a complete cooling before slicing to allow the crumb to fully set. This recipe produces two loaves, making it perfect for your weekend batch-baking activities. For freezing tips, see page 15.

The addition of bananas in the leaven is inspired by the experimentation of many Japanese bakers who use yeast waters made from fermenting fresh or dried fruits or by adding fruit to slightly influence their leaven with subtle character. Although only slightly noticeable, the mashed banana adds an unparalleled flavor to the dough that smells wonderfully exotic from the mixing to the finished bake. If you do not have buttermilk on hand, you may substitute whole-milk yogurt instead. (Recipe shown on page 31.)

FOR THE SOURDOUGH LEAVEN

1 large, very ripe banana (about 125 g)
50 g / 2 tablespoons 100% hydration active
    sourdough starter, refreshed (page 10)
50 g / 5 tablespoons water (70°F)
50 g / ½ cup whole rye flour

FOR THE SOAKER

20 g / 2 tablespoons whole flax seeds
55 g / ¼ cup water (70°F)

FOR THE DOUGH

465 g / 1¾ cups plus 2 tablespoons whole
    buttermilk
225 g / 1 cup water (75°F)
45 g / 2 heaping tablespoons maple syrup
20 g / 4 teaspoons fine sea salt
800 g / 7½ cups plus 1 tablespoon whole
    rye flour
200 g / 1¾ cups Type T-85 wheat flour
    (high extraction bread flour)
Butter or oil for greasing a tin (if using)

FOR THE TOPPING

20 to 30 g / 2 to 3 tablespoons whole flax seeds
    (optional)

PREPARE THE LEAVEN AND SOAKER

To build the leaven, mash the banana in a large bowl using a fork—a few small remaining lumps are OK. Add the starter and water and stir. Stir in the flour until the mixture is well hydrated and somewhat soupy. Cover and leave to ferment at room temperature until puffy and aromatic, 8 to 12 hours.

To prepare the soaker, place the flax seeds in a separate small bowl and add the water. Cover and allow to rest at room temperature until you are ready to mix the dough.

MIX THE DOUGH

To the bowl with the leaven, add the soaker, buttermilk, water, maple syrup, and salt and stir to a slurry. Add the flours and mix using your hands until the dough is well-hydrated and no lumps remain. It will feel extremely sticky due to the nature of whole rye flour and the hydrated flax seeds.

Cover and allow the dough to bulk proof at room temperature for 3 to 4 hours, depending on the ambient temperature of your kitchen. Stretch and fold the dough 3 to 4 times, about once per hour. The dough will not visibly rise or increase in volume during bulk proofing, but it should feel puffy and alive when ready to shape.

SHAPE THE DOUGH

To shape the loaves, divide the dough into 2 equal pieces and choose your preferred shaping method. Prepare the tins by rubbing them generously with butter. Alternatively, generously flour 1 or 2 linen-lined proofing baskets, depending on the desired loaf size.

If shaping the dough into loaf tins, wet your fingers to prevent sticking, then transfer the dough to the tins, pressing gently to fill the gaps and corners. Using a small amount of water, slick down the tops of the loaves until the surface is smooth and even. Top with a generous sprinkling of flax seeds and cover with linen and then plastic; refrigerate the loaves overnight.

If preparing hearth loaves, generously coat your hands with flour or water to prevent sticking. Coax the loaves into an even, round form by pulling the sides into the middle until a loose seam forms. Place the loaves into the floured, lined baskets, seam-sides up. Cover with linen and then plastic and refrigerate the loaves overnight.

BAKE

Pull the loaves from the refrigerator 2 hours prior to baking, and allow them to come to room temperature. They will have only slightly risen in the tins or baskets overnight.

If baking in tins: Preheat the oven to 475°F. Place a rack in the middle of the oven and a roasting pan on the second rack just below. Carefully pour about ½ cup of water into the roasting pan and place the loaves on the middle rack in the oven. Bake with steam for 12 to 15 minutes, then lower the temperature to 425°F. Continue to bake for another 50 to 55 minutes or until the crust is a deep dark, bold brown.

If using a Dutch oven (preferably enamel coated): Place the Dutch oven on the middle rack and preheat to 480°F for 20 minutes. Sprinkle a touch of cornmeal onto a piece of parchment paper cut to fit the bottom of the Dutch oven, and carefully transfer one loaf onto it, seam-side up. (This will allow the seam to open and expand during baking, eliminating the need to score the loaf.) Bake with the lid on for 20 minutes. Remove the lid, lower the temperature to 425°F, and continue baking for another 40 to 45 minutes, tipping the bread out directly onto the oven rack after 20 minutes if your oven runs hot or if you are using a non-enameled cast iron Dutch oven. Repeat with the remaining loaf.

COOL

Tip the loaves from the tins or remove the round loaf from the Dutch oven and allow to cool completely on a wire rack before slicing. This gives the crumb a chance to fully set and prevent a gummy texture that is possible when baking breads high in rye flour. If you can manage patience, it is even better when left to cool overnight.

TRY IT WITH . . . Slice thinly to serve with cured meats or fish such as **Beet-Cured Gravlax** or **Baccalà Mantecato**. Top with **Crème Fraîche** before garnishing with **Pickled Shrimp**. It is delicious served with **Labneh** swirled with your favorite jam, or **Blushing Goat Spread** topped with chopped dried fruit and nuts or savory garnishes such as green onion, fresh herbs, and **Citrus Salt**.

Black Bread

— MAKES 1 LOAF —

Although this bread resembles pumpernickel, the use of mostly wheat flour makes it untraditional in its formulation. Slightly sweet and rich in flavor with notes of coffee and chocolate, this Black Bread sports a wonderfully open crumb and beautiful, thick and somewhat smoky crust when baked in a Dutch oven, or it can be shaped into a tin loaf and baked at 435°F for a softer, thinner crust. Both methods yield a medium crumb perfect for enjoying with all manner of toppings. (Recipe shown on pages 130, 220.)

90 g / scant ½ cup 100% hydration active sourdough starter, refreshed (page 10)

225 g / 1 cup water (70°F)

115 g / ½ cup strongly brewed coffee, tepid

40 g / 2 tablespoons unsulphured molasses

280 g / 2 cups bread flour

115 g / 1 cup whole wheat flour

55 g / ½ cup medium rye flour

10 g / 2 tablespoons cocoa powder

10 g / 2 teaspoons fine sea salt

Butter or oil for greasing a tin (if using)

MIX THE DOUGH

Place the starter, water, coffee, and molasses in a large bowl and stir to a slurry. Slowly incorporate the flours, using your hands to mix until a shaggy dough forms with no dry lumps remaining. Cover the bowl and allow the dough to autolyze at room temperature for 20 to 30 minutes.

Sprinkle the salt over the dough and mix with your hands to distribute it evenly. Remove the dough from the bowl and perform the slap-and-fold method on a clean surface.

Clean and lightly oil your bowl and return the dough. Cover the bowl and allow the dough to bulk proof at room temperature for about 4 hours, stretching and folding every 30 to 45 minutes to further build strength in the dough.

SHAPE THE DOUGH

Once the dough has increased in size by at least one-third and feels springy and elastic to the touch, remove it from the bowl and preshape it into your desired form (round if baking in a Dutch oven or rectangular if baking in a tin). Cover loosely with plastic or a damp towel and allow the loaf to relax for 10 to 30 minutes before performing the final shaping.

If shaping into a boule, pull the dough into the middle of the loaf to create surface tension. Pinch the seam closed and place it in a proofing basket, seam-side up. Cover with a dry cloth and then plastic, then place the basket in the refrigerator for 8 to 36 hours.

If you are baking in a loaf tin, follow the instructions for shaping and baking the Pain de Mie (page 57).

BAKE

Remove the loaf from the refrigerator and allow it to come to room temperature for about 1 hour. In the meantime, preheat a Dutch oven (preferably enamel coated) to 490°F for 20 minutes. Sprinkle a touch of cornmeal onto a piece of parchment paper cut to fit the bottom of the Dutch oven and carefully flip your loaf onto it, seam-side down. Score the top of the loaf about ¼ to ½ inch deep with a razor blade. Carefully lower the parchment paper and loaf into the preheated Dutch oven, position the lid, and return it to the oven. Reduce the temperature to 480°F and bake with the lid on for 20 minutes. Remove the lid, reduce the oven temperature to 475°F, and bake for another 15 minutes, tipping the loaf out of the Dutch oven and directly onto the oven rack after about 7 minutes if your oven runs hot or if you are baking in a non-enameled cast iron pot. Cool the bread completely on a wire rack before slicing.

TRY IT WITH . . . The unique and bold flavor of this bread is delicious served with soft butter and **Vanilla Marmalade** or **Tomato Marmalade**. It is an excellent sandwich or tartine choice, especially when paired with **Horseradish Apple Cream** and **Baccalà Mantecato**. For a simple appetizer, slice the bread into small wedges, smear with **Crème Fraîche**, and adorn with sustainably sourced roe or **Beet-Cured Gravlax** and a sprinkling of fresh dill. It is wonderful drizzled with extra-virgin olive oil and toasted on the grill.

Spiced Carrot Levain

— MAKES 1 LOAF —

This naturally leavened bread has a mildly sweet carrot flavor and a lovely, blushed crumb color as a result of using fresh carrot juice to hydrate the dough. I prefer it spiced with aromatic seeds, but if you prefer a more neutral bread, simply omit the seeds for a crusty hearth loaf with a slight hint of sweet carrot. Alternatively, triple the amounts of the seeds and use them untoasted to coat the outside of the shaped loaf for a textural presentation. This is a moderately hydrated dough, easy to work and shape, but if you desire a more open crumb, increase the carrot juice by 25 to 40 grams.

1 teaspoon cumin seeds (optional)

1 teaspoon coriander seeds (optional)

1 teaspoon caraway seeds (optional)

120 g / ½ cup plus scant tablespoon
   100% hydration active sourdough starter,
   refreshed (page 10)

375 g / 1½ cups plus 1½ tablespoons fresh
   carrot juice (70°F)

350 g / 2½ cups bread flour

100 g / ¾ cup plus 2 tablespoons
   whole wheat flour

50 g / ½ cup medium rye flour

10 g / 2 teaspoons fine sea salt

MIX THE DOUGH

If you are using the seeds, toast them in a dry skillet and then crush them using a mortar and pestle. Set them aside.

Place the starter and carrot juice in a large bowl and stir to form a slurry. Slowly incorporate the flours and optional seeds, using your hands to mix until a shaggy dough forms with no dry lumps remaining. Cover the bowl and allow the dough to autolyze at room temperature for 20 to 30 minutes.

Sprinkle the salt over the dough and mix with your hands to distribute it evenly. Remove the dough from the bowl and perform a series of slap-and-folds on a clean work surface.

Clean and lightly oil your bowl and return the dough. Cover the bowl and allow the dough to bulk proof at room temperature for about 3 to 4 hours, stretching and folding every 30 to 45 minutes to further build strength in the dough.

SHAPE THE DOUGH

Once the dough has increased in size by at least one-third and feels springy and elastic to the touch, remove it from the bowl and preshape it into your desired form. Cover and allow the dough to relax for 10 to 30 minutes before performing the final shaping, pulling the

dough into itself to create surface tension. Place it in a proofing basket, seam-side up, cover with a cloth and then plastic, and place it in the refrigerator for 8 to 24 hours.

BAKE

Remove the loaf from the refrigerator and allow it to come to room temperature for about 1 hour.

Preheat a Dutch oven (preferably enamel coated) to 500°F for 20 minutes. Sprinkle a touch of cornmeal onto a piece of parchment paper cut to fit the bottom of the Dutch oven and carefully flip your loaf onto it, seam-side down. Score the top of the loaf about ¼ to ½ inch deep with a razor blade or lame. Carefully lower the parchment paper and loaf into the preheated Dutch oven, position the lid, and return it to the oven. Reduce the oven temperature to 480°F and bake with the lid on for 20 minutes. Remove the lid and bake for another 12 to 20 minutes until the crust is brown.

TRY IT WITH . . . This bread is surprisingly versatile and is appropriate served with either sweet or savory toppings. Snuggle it up to **Warm Brussels Sprouts Salad**; dunk it into a quality olive oil before dipping into **Dukkah**; adorn with **Ramp and Carrot Top Pesto Spread**; or smear with **Labneh** and **Gingered Sweet Potato Butter** or **Gingered Guava and Chili Preserves**.

KITCHEN NOTE I prefer my bottom crust as thick and dark as possible, but if you are using a cast-iron pot, you will need to tip the loaf out of the Dutch oven after about 25 minutes of baking time to prevent the bottom from burning before the loaf is fully baked. This must be done carefully to avoid burning yourself. Finish baking the loaf directly on the middle rack for an additional 12 to 20 minutes, depending on your crust preference.

THE ART OF TOAST

The flavor or aroma of "toast" can be detected in a vast collection of foods, from a baguette to a marshmallow, a steak, or sesame seeds. When bread is the choice ingredient, the process of toasting is a distinctive and pleasing olfactory experience, making it a quintessential comfort food to be enjoyed any time in the day.

Just what exactly happens when we slice a piece of bread and subject it to heat? The molecular components of bread undergo a beautiful transformation, first smelled during the initial baking time. A chemical process called the Maillard Reaction occurs between simple sugars and amino acids that have been subjected to the heat. This reaction visibly darkens the bread and produces flavor compounds responsible for elevating your morning breakfast routine or quick lunch fix into an aromatically indulgent experience. If you're a weekend baker, your beautiful Sunday loaf can feed you every morning thereafter without the sacrifice of freshness. Here are a few of my favorite methods for making perfect toast.

DRY TOAST

Although you are certainly welcome to toast your bread under the broiler, if you are easily distracted like me, the fire alarm usually signals smoke and flame before you even notice the bread has browned! Have a little patience and follow the steps below for an even, dry toast that is ready to absorb whatever you choose as a pairing.

Preheat your oven to 425°F. Lay the slices of bread on an unlined sheet pan and place it on the middle rack. Toast well or to your preferred taste, at least 5 minutes for the crumb to begin gaining in color. Watch (and sniff) carefully thereafter.

SKILLET TOAST

This method of practically frying bread is delicious for perking up particularly stale slices or for serving with fruits or vegetables that could benefit from the more robust mouthfeel of a little fat. If you're feeling particularly indulgent, substitute the oil with bacon or duck fat. Mmmm, duck fat skillet toast . . .

In a large heavy-bottomed skillet or griddle, melt 1½ tablespoons of unsalted butter with 1½ tablespoons of olive oil over medium-low heat until the butter is bubbly. Lower the heat and place 3 to 4 slices of bread flat in the skillet. Fry each side for 3 to 4 minutes or until golden brown. Remove the toast and serve it immediately or transfer to a preheated 250°F oven to keep it warm. Repeat with more butter, olive oil, and bread slices.

MAYONNAISE MAGIC SKILLET TOAST

The proteins and rich fats that come from both the oil and eggs in mayonnaise are unparalleled even to butter for browning bread in the skillet. Use this method to prepare open-faced tartines or to make The Best Grilled Cheese Sandwich (see below), which sports a crisp outer layer with a soft inner crumb, buttery flavor, and gooey middle. It is comfort food at its best!

Evenly smear mayonnaise onto both sides of each piece of bread. Heat ½ tablespoon unsalted butter and ½ tablespoon oil in a heavy-bottomed skillet over medium heat until the butter is melted. Swirl the pan to coat and place the bread in the skillet. Fry for 2 to 3 minutes on each side or until your desired color is achieved.

THE BEST GRILLED CHEESE SANDWICH

There is no substitute for the satisfaction of the perfect union between toasted bread and melty cheese. Using mayonnaise as your toasting medium gives a crispy, perfectly browned foil for your cheese and toppings of choice. Following the instructions for the Mayonnaise Magic Skillet Toast (see above), heat the butter and oil in a heavy-bottomed skillet over medium heat. Use only 1 to 1½ tablespoons of mayonnaise to smear onto one side of each piece of bread. Slather the other sides with the condiment of your choice (perhaps more mayonnaise!) or leave it plain.

Turn the heat to the lowest setting and place one piece of bread, mayonnaise-side down, into the pan. Top with ½ cup of grated hard cheese of your choice or several chunks of room-temperature triple cream cheese. (This would be an excellent time to add sliced apples, mashed avocado, fresh berries, or a fermented vegetable.) Lay the other bread slice over the cheese, mayonnaise-side up, and heat until you see the cheese just beginning to melt. Check the bottom for browning, and using a spatula, quickly flip to the other side. Continue heating until the cheese has melted through and the bread is a deep golden brown on both sides. Serve warm.

The possibilities for creating a unique and satisfying melty sandwich can lean in either the sweet or savory direction; here are a few suggestions to get your imagination flowing:

- Cheddar with **Cranberry, Apricot, and Apple Mostarda**
- Brie with **Caramel Apple Bourbon Butter**
- Muenster with bacon and **Onion, Thyme, and Date Jam**
- Muenster or mozzarella with **Gingered Guava and Chili Preserves**
- Swiss with **Fermented Grainy Mustard** and a slice of tomato
- Pepper Jack with **Tomato Marmalade**
- Gruyère with **Herb Jam**
- Comté with fresh figs or **Thyme-Roasted Pears with Red Onion and Gorgonzola**

Moonbread

My personal preference for bread that accommodates jam is one that has a moderate crumb, perfect for ample slathering without losing precious dollops of goodness on my lap. Occasionally, though, a bread for sopping up sauce or quality olive oil is more than necessary. Traditional ciabatta, or the northern Italian "slipper bread" named for its appearance, is one such bread that I adore even though it's typically made with high amounts of refined white flour. I tested my way through many versions before finally coming to this einkorn-enhanced beauty with a robust flavor. If you cannot source einkorn, replace with spelt or even whole wheat flour in a pinch.

While finishing this manuscript, I moved to the seaside and became more sensitive than ever to the pull of the moon and its effect on the tides; the appearance of this loaf feels like an expression of this cycle. A well-hydrated dough, it requires a hefty amount of flour upon final shaping and proofing. The result is a beautiful lunar landscape on the surface with an open, soft crumb reminiscent of the many faces of the moon. (Recipe shown on page 228.)

FOR THE SOURDOUGH LEAVEN

50 g / 2 tablespoons 100% hydration active
    sourdough starter, refreshed (page 10)
50 g / 5 tablespoons water (75°F)
50 g / scant ½ cup whole einkorn flour

FOR THE DOUGH

375 g / 1½ cups plus 4 tablespoons water (75°F)
25 g / 1 tablespoon plus 2 teaspoons extra-virgin
    olive oil
100 g / scant 1 cup whole einkorn flour
400 g / 3⅓ cups all-purpose flour
10 g / 2 teaspoons fine sea salt

MIX THE LEAVEN

Place the starter and water in a large bowl and stir to a slurry. Stir in the flour until well hydrated. Cover and allow the leaven to ferment at room temperature until bubbly and aromatic, 8 to 12 hours.

MIX THE DOUGH

To the bowl with the leaven, add the water, stir in the oil, and then add the flours. Mix with your hands until a shaggy dough forms and no dry lumps remain. Cover the bowl and allow the dough to autolyze at room temperature for 20 to 30 minutes.

Sprinkle in the salt and mix with your hands to distribute it evenly and work it into the dough.

Remove the dough from the bowl. Clean the bowl and lightly coat it with oil, then return the dough. Gently toss to coat and cover with plastic. Let the dough bulk proof at room temperature for about 3 hours, stretching and folding every 30 to 45 minutes. Cover with a towel and then plastic and place the bowl in the refrigerator for 8 to 12 hours.

SHAPE THE DOUGH

There are various ways to shape ciabatta dough into its characteristic slipper shape, but using this technique ensures that the dough is handled gently. Prepare a baker's couche by laying it flat and flouring it heavily. Also prepare a work surface by flouring it heavily. Swiftly empty the dough onto the very well-floured work surface. Gently stretch it into a rectangular shape about 1½ inches thick, being careful not to deflate the dough. Divide the dough into 3 pieces for large loaves or 9 pieces for ciabatta rolls. Gently transfer each piece onto the floured couche, bunching the fabric up in between each loaf to provide support and to prevent them from sticking together. Dust generously with flour and cover loosely with plastic. Allow to finish proofing in a warm location for about 1½ to 2 hours or until the loaves appear puffy with multiple air bubbles rising to the surface.

BAKE

About 45 minutes before the loaves are ready to bake, place a hearthstone on the middle rack of your oven and place a roasting pan on the rack beneath it. Preheat the oven to 500°F. Sprinkle a peel with cornmeal or semolina flour, or cover the peel or the underside of a sheet pan with a piece of parchment paper no larger than your hearthstone, and then sprinkle it with cornmeal or semolina flour. Place the proofed ciabatta loaves on the prepared peel or sheet pan, leaving at least 3½ inches between the larger loaves. Carefully pour about ½ cup (115 g) of water into the preheated roasting pan to create steam. Quickly load the ciabatta into the oven, sliding the loaves and parchment (if using) onto the hearthstone. Close the oven door and bake for about 5 minutes, then reduce the oven temperature to 480°F. Continue baking for about 20 minutes or until the loaves are a deep golden brown and sound hollow when thumped on the bottom. Let them cool completely on a wire rack.

TRY IT WITH . . . The structure of this bread is perfect for sopping up **Roasted Cherry Tomato Confit** or topping with **Labneh** and **Grilled Escarole** or **Sorghum-Roasted Carrots**, **Tahini Sauce**, and **Dukkah**. To create a toasted sandwich, smash some **Garlic and Sun-Dried Tomato Confit** onto the inside crumb. Top with **Onion, Thyme, and Date Jam** or a cheese of your choice and sautéed greens before placing in a preheated 400°F oven until the cheese has melted.

KITCHEN NOTE Using a long, thin board a few inches wider and longer than the ciabatta can help to easily and gently transfer them to the peel or parchment paper–lined sheet pan. Position the board next to the proofed loaves, and using the couche fabric to assist, flip them onto the board. It will then be quite easy to slip them onto the peel.

A Modest Baguette

— MAKES 4 SMALL BAGUETTES OR TORDU —

I have always considered baguettes to be one of the simplest yet most difficult breads to make. They require a delicate balance between a crisp crust and a chewy crumb. There should be a well-developed, creamy flavor, perfect shaping and scoring, and a particular lightness to the bake. Mostly, I have left this fussy challenge to the expertise of commercial retail bakeries and their fancy steam-injected ovens, rather than trying to replicate them myself. But one particular night in Cali, Colombia, left me with a renewed enthusiasm to calculate a formula.

Salsa dancing was never something I aspired to master, and I was rather intimidated upon the solicitation of several fellow tourists in a city most known for its incredible salsa clubs. Along with a German, a Frenchman, and an Argentinian, I figured I wouldn't be the only awkward *gringa* on the dancefloor, though, so I relented. Much to my surprise, there was no judgment from the many accomplished locals, who I wrongly assumed would rather laugh than take the time to teach me the steps. I was whirled around by several dance partners until delightfully dizzy. As the sun filled the cobblestone streets, we walked back through the quiet San Antonio neighborhood to our little guesthouse, famished and elated with dancing joy. I lamented to the Frenchman about the situation of mediocre bread in South America and how at that moment the only thing that could make me happier would be a good, crusty baguette. I hopped into the shower while the others prepared breakfast, and upon joining the table, there laid a most modest baguette, perfectly adequate to satisfy our morning hunger.

This formula allows you to create your own rustic baguettes at home, but honestly I prefer to shape them into tordu, or what the French fancifully call "twisted." Included are instructions for shaping and scoring this loose dough into demi-baguettes. I, however, strongly suggest that you crank some salsa music or even Serge Gainsbourg through the speakers as a soundtrack for skipping the technical baguette bravado. Free-form the dough instead into beautifully organic tordu shapes.

The following fermentation schedule is inspired by master baker Ian Lowe of Tasmania, who uses a cold bulk ferment mixed in the early morning to have loaves ready to fuel an evening of dancing or entertaining. Natural leavening achieves the flavor of a traditional baguette, and low-protein flours ensure that the texture is not too chewy with a beautifully open, golden crumb. (If you cannot source stone-ground einkorn flour, replace it with whole spelt flour instead.) This dough is also excellent made into a flavorful pizza crust, sprinkled with sesame seeds before baking at 500°F on a preheated hearthstone.

FOR THE SOURDOUGH LEAVEN

50 g / 2 tablespoons 100% hydration active
    sourdough starter, refreshed (page 10)

50 g / 5 tablespoons water (75°F)

50 g / ⅓ cup bread flour

FOR THE DOUGH

405 g / 1⅔ cups plus 3 tablespoons water (75°F)

20 g / 1 tablespoon barley malt syrup

230 g / 1⅔ cups bread flour

215 g / 2 cups "00" flour

180 g / 1⅔ cups whole einkorn flour

12 g / 2½ teaspoons fine sea salt

PREPARE THE SOURDOUGH LEAVEN

Place the starter and water in a large mixing bowl and stir to a slurry. Stir in the flour until well hydrated. Cover the bowl and let the leaven ferment at room temperature until bubbly and fragrant, 8 to 12 hours.

MIX THE DOUGH

Pour the water into a large mixing bowl and add the flours. Mix with your hands until a shaggy dough forms with no dry lumps remaining. Cover the bowl and allow the dough to autolyze at room temperature for 1 to 4 hours. Add the sourdough leaven and salt and continue mixing with your hands until the leaven and salt are evenly distributed and no streaks remain. Remove the dough from the bowl. Clean and lightly oil the bowl, then return the dough to it. Gently toss to coat, then cover the bowl with plastic. Leave to bulk proof at room tempera-ture for about 1 hour, stretching and folding every 20 minutes in the bowl. Cover with a dry towel and then plastic and bulk proof in the refrigerator for 6 to 10 hours.

SHAPE THE DOUGH

Gently remove the dough from the bowl. It will feel slack, sticky, and somewhat loose.

    Divide the dough into four equal parts and gently pat each one into a rough rectangle. Fold one-third of each dough rectangle into the center and then roll to fold downward again, gently patting the seam closed. Turn the preshaped dough pieces so they are positioned seam-sides down, then cover them with a towel and allow them to rest for about 20 min-utes, until the dough relaxes and returns to room temperature.

    To make demi-baguettes or tordu, final shape by turning each over onto a generously floured work surface, seam-side up. Using your bench knife to assist, fold the top third of the dough to the middle and then fold the bottom third toward the middle, slightly over-lapping the two. Use the heel of your hand to firmly press and seal the seams. Repeat this process, folding the top half down to the center and using the heel of your hand to press and seal along the seam as you tuck the dough with your other hand to create tension. Work this folded portion again toward the bottom, tucking and folding with each roll until a long, tight cylinder is created. Seal the final seam firmly with the heel of your hand. Finish shaping the baguette by rolling it into a coil that fits the length of your baking stone, tapering it toward the ends. Repeat with the remaining preshaped dough pieces.

Place the shaped loaves into a well-floured baker's couche, seam-sides up, bunching the fabric between the loaves and supporting the sides. (Or you could place them seam-side down into baguette tins.) Cover with plastic and allow to final proof for 1 to 1½ hours before performing the poke test. Alternatively, once shaped, you may cover the loaves with plastic and place the baguettes in the refrigerator for 2 to 3 hours before baking for improved flavor.

BAKE

About 45 minutes before the loaves are ready to bake, position a hearthstone on the middle rack of your oven with a roasting pan on the rack underneath. Preheat the oven to 500°F.

Place a piece of parchment paper on a peel or the back of a sheet pan and dust it lightly with cornmeal or coarse semolina flour. Swiftly transfer the loaves to the parchment, seam-side down, leaving about 3 inches between each loaf. Score each loaf with a razor blade, making one ¼-inch-deep cut that runs the length of the loaf at a 45-degree angle. If making into tordus, skip the scoring and twist each end in opposite directions, creating an organic, wiggly shape. Carefully pour about ½ cup (115 g) of water into the preheated roasting pan to create steam. Slide the parchment onto the preheated hearthstone and bake with steam for the first 7 to 10 minutes, spraying the tops of the loaves with a water bottle inter-mittently if you have one handy. (Be careful not to spray the oven light!) Reduce the oven temperature to 480°F and continue baking for another 15 minutes or until the crust is light golden brown. Remove the baguettes from the oven and let them cool completely on a wire rack.

TRY IT WITH . . . Baguettes or tordu are best eaten the day they are baked, served with any number of sweet or savory spreads. They also make delicious Vietnamese-style sandwiches layered with **Homemade Mayonnaise**, pâté, sliced jalapeño, **Quickles** of carrots and onions, and fresh cilantro. Slice thinly to make them into **Garlic Crostini**. The twisted crunchy heels are fun to tear and dip into any number of flavored oils or sauces such as aioli.

> **KITCHEN NOTE** Using a long, thin board a few inches wider and longer than the baguettes can help to easily and gently transfer them to the parchment paper–lined sheet pan or peel. Position the board next to the proofed loaves and, using the couche fabric to assist, flip them onto the board. It will be quite easy to slip them onto the peel or sheet pan.

Pain de Mie

— MAKES 1 LARGE LOAF —

As much as I love a hearth loaf with a thick and crusty caramelized exterior, sometimes I crave the yield of a lighter, soft and spongy bread. This recipe draws inspiration from Julia Child's revered Pain de Mie recipe but includes the use of both sourdough starter and yogurt. This is what I consider the perfect sandwich loaf for kids, with a toothsome result, long shelf-life, and tangy, robust flavor. Make sure to work with room temperature ingredients to ensure a good, even mix. If you wish for a more nutritious bread and can source whole einkorn flour, try substituting it for one-third of the all-purpose flour. The resulting bread will have a significantly more robust flavor and beautiful golden crumb, and it will be easier to digest, too.

115 g / ½ cup whole milk

30 g / 1½ tablespoons mild honey

1 teaspoon active dry yeast (optional)

180 g / ¾ cup plain whole-milk yogurt

100 g / ½ cup 100% hydration active sourdough
    starter, refreshed (page 10)

360 g / 3 cups all-purpose flour

60 g / ½ cup Type T-85 hard wheat
    (high-extraction bread flour)

45 g / 3 tablespoons unsalted butter,
    cubed and softened

8 g / 1½ teaspoons fine sea salt

Butter or oil for greasing the tin

FOR THE WASH

15 g / ½ tablespoon whole milk

MIX THE DOUGH

Combine the milk and honey in a medium saucepan over low heat and cook gently for about 3 to 4 minutes, stirring until the honey is dissolved. Remove the pan from the heat, sprinkle in the yeast, and set the pan aside for about 10 minutes to allow the yeast to activate and proof.

Meanwhile, combine the yogurt and starter in a large bowl. Pour in the milk mixture and stir to a slurry. Add the flour, working with your hands until everything is hydrated and no lumps remain. The dough will be fairly sticky. Cover the bowl and allow the dough to autolyze for about 20 minutes.

Remove the dough from the bowl and place onto a clean work surface. Sprinkle the salt over the dough and work in the butter using the palm of your hand to smear the butter into the dough against the counter. Once the butter is incorporated, knead the dough on a lightly floured work surface for an additional 10 minutes or until the dough becomes an

elastic, smooth mass. Clean the bowl and place the dough back in it. Cover the bowl and allow the dough to bulk proof until it takes on a marshmallow consistency and has at least doubled in size, 2½ to 3 hours if using commercial yeast, 4½ to 5 hours if using only sourdough leavening.

Remove the dough from the bowl, place it on a lightly floured work surface, and pat it into a rectangle about 2 inches thick. Fold the dough over itself several times, then place it back in the bowl to proof for an additional 1 to 1½ hours. Alternatively, skip this step if using sourdough leavening only and continue bulk proofing.

SHAPE THE DOUGH

Generously grease a loaf tin and set it aside.

When the dough has doubled its size, remove it from the bowl, place it on a lightly floured work surface, and pat it into a rectangle. Return the dough to the bowl, seam-side down, cover, and allow it to bench rest for about 10 minutes.

Place the dough on a lightly floured work surface with the seam of the rectangle facing up, and fold the top third of the rectangle to the center, using the heel of your hand to seal the seam. Fold the bottom third of the rectangle to the center, overlapping the first fold only slightly and again sealing the seam with the heel of your hand. Now fold the dough in half, tucking with one hand and sealing with the heel of the other hand to gain some increased tension. Generously grease a loaf tin with butter or oil. Place the dough into the greased tin, seam-side down, firmly patting the top and coaxing the dough into the corners if needed. Cover and allow to proof in a warm location until the loaf barely crests the top of the tin, 30 minutes to 1 hour, depending on the season or ambient temperature of your kitchen. If using sourdough leavening only, final proof for 1½ to 2 hours or until the loaf barely crests the top of the tin.

BAKE

Preheat the oven to 435°F. Brush the loaf lightly with the milk wash and score the top with a razor blade or lame, making a ¼-inch-deep slit down the center. Bake for about 30 to 35 minutes. The loaf will be done when the sides pull away from the tin and the loaf gives a hollow thud when tapped on the top.

Remove from the oven and slip the loaf from the pan. Although the aroma will tempt you, allow the bread to cool completely on a wire rack before slicing.

TRY IT WITH . . . This bread is perfect for **Mayonnaise Magic Skillet Toast** and **The Best Grilled Cheese Sandwich**. Lightly toast and spread slices with **Crème Fraîche**, cucumber slices, fresh chives, and borage flowers for afternoon tea. Pair it with **Matcha Nut Butter**, **Cinnamon-Hazelnut Butter**, or **Roasted Banana and Chocolate Nut Butter** and top with fresh fruit. Use this bread to make a light and custardy version of **Baked Pain Perdu**.

KITCHEN NOTE Tin loaves can sometimes appear misshapen as a result of over- or under-proofing. If the top of your loaf appears to have blown off or looks like it is trying to fly away, this is a result of underproofing. Next time, during the final proof after the loaf is formed and placed in the tin, simply allow for a longer rise before you bake the bread. Alternatively, if your loaf comes out of the oven looking sunken and deflated, this is a result of overproof-ing. Next time, allow it a shorter final rise before baking.

Buckwheat Milk Bread

— MAKES 2 LOAVES —

This rich, brioche-like bread has an incomparably soft crumb that is unlike anything else you will bake from this book. Inspired by the Japanese-style milk breads, this formula gelatinizes milk and flour into a paste called tangzhong (similiar to a roux) that is then added to the dough. The result is a feathery bread with the slightly earthy aroma of buckwheat. This recipe uses a Pullman pan to make square loaves, but you can just as easily shape the dough into round rolls and stuff them into loaf tins to create a pull-apart bread. If using sourdough leavening only, increase the amount of leavening to 150 g / ¾ cup and be prepared for a slightly different flavor and heavier texture.

FOR THE TANGZHONG

45 g / ⅓ cup bread flour

115 g / ½ cup whole milk

115 g / ½ cup water

FOR THE WASH

20 g / 1½ tablespoons whole milk

FOR THE DOUGH

230 g / 1 cup whole milk (100°F)

60 g / 3 tablespoons buckwheat or dark honey

1 teaspoon active dry yeast (optional)

2 large eggs (100 g), lightly beaten

100 g / ½ cup 100% hydration active sourdough
    starter, refreshed (page 10)

630 g / 4½ cups bread flour

30 g / ¼ cup buckwheat flour

85 g / 6 tablespoons unsalted butter, softened

15 g / 3 teaspoons fine sea salt

Butter or oil for greasing the tins

MIX THE DOUGH

To make the tangzhong, whisk together the flour, milk, and water in a medium saucepan until smooth. Place the pan over medium-low heat and whisk constantly until the mixture thickens but is still pourable, about 3 to 4 minutes. (Do not walk away, as this transformation will happen very quickly!) Transfer the mixture to a large bowl and allow it to cool.

To make the dough, place the warm milk in a small bowl and stir in the honey. Sprinkle in the yeast (if using), and allow the mixture to proof for about 10 minutes.

Transfer the yeast mixture to the large bowl with the tangzhong and stir in the eggs and starter to form a smooth slurry. Add the flours and mix with your hands until the dough is well hydrated and no lumps remain. The dough will be very sticky. Cover the bowl and allow the dough to autolyze at room temperature for 20 minutes.

Add the butter and sprinkle in the salt, mixing with your hands to incorporate both into the dough. Once the ingredients are evenly distributed, remove the dough from the bowl and gently knead it on a well-floured counter for 3 to 5 minutes, adding a touch of flour if necessary, until somewhat smooth dough is achieved. Clean and lightly oil the bowl and return the dough to it. Cover the bowl and allow the dough to bulk proof at room temperature until it has tripled in size, about 3 hours. If using sourdough leavening only, bulk proof the dough for 4½ to 5 hours or until it has almost doubled in size.

SHAPE THE DOUGH

Generously grease two 9 × 4-inch Pullman or loaf tins, including the lids. Transfer the dough from the bowl to a lightly floured work surface. Divide it into 2 equal pieces and fold them into even rectangles. Place the rectangles seam-sides down on the work surface, cover, and allow them to bench rest for about 10 minutes.

Flip the dough rectangles so the seam sides are facing up. Fold the top third of each rectangle to the center, using the heel of your hand to seal the seam. Fold the bottom third of each rectangle to the center, overlapping the first fold only slightly and again sealing the seam with the heel of your hand. Now fold the dough in half, tucking with one hand and sealing with the heel of your other hand to gain some increased tension. Place the formed dough into the greased tins, seam-sides down, firmly patting the top and coaxing the dough into the corners if needed. Cover with plastic or the Pullman lids and allow to proof in a warm location until the loaves have barely crested the top of the tins, about 1½ hours (or 2½ to 3 hours if using sourdough leavening only).

BAKE

Preheat the oven to 375°F. If baking in tins without lids, brush the loaves lightly with the milk wash and score the top of each loaf with a razor blade or lame, making a ¼-inch-deep slit down the center. It is not necessary to score the Pullman loaf; simply bake it with the lid on. Bake for about 30 to 40 minutes in an uncovered tin or 35 minutes in a covered Pullman pan. The loaves will be done when the sides pull away from the tins and the crusts are golden brown on top. Remove from the oven and allow to rest for 5 to 7 minutes before slipping the loaves from the pans. Although the aroma will tempt you, allow the bread to cool completely on a wire rack before slicing.

TRY IT WITH . . . This bread is excellent served with bright, red fruit jams, **Gingered Sweet Potato Butter**, or a light smear of softened butter.

KITCHEN NOTE Tin loaves can sometimes appear misshapen as a result of over- or under-proofing. If the top of your loaf appears to have blown off or looks like it is trying to fly away, this is a result of underproofing. Next time, during the final proof after the loaf is formed and placed in the tin, simply allow for a longer rise before you bake the bread. Alternatively, if your loaf comes out of the oven looking sunken and deflated, this is a result of overproofing. Next time, allow it a shorter final rise before baking.

Oat Flour Brioche

— MAKES 12 SMALL BUNS OR 1 TIN LOAF —

Most brioche doughs call for flour that is rather low in gluten protein, which helps it develop a golden brown, pillowy soft bun. In developing this recipe, I wanted to include a significant amount of whole grains but also maintain the light, buttery soft crumb that is so characteristic of brioche. Oat flour was a natural choice, since it contains no gluten at all and has a naturally sweet flavor when baked, and combined with a touch of honey and the rich contribution of eggs and butter, it produced the morning buns of my dreams! This dough can also be made into a loaf, using the shaping method for Pain de Mie on page 59. (Recipe shown on page 132.)

---

80 g / 6 tablespoons whole milk (100°F)

40 g / 2 tablespoons mild honey

1½ teaspoons active dry yeast

150 g / 1½ cups 100% hydration active
    sourdough starter, refreshed (page 10)

8 egg yolks (130 g), lightly beaten

240 g / 2 cups all-purpose flour

150 g / 1½ cups oat flour

115 g / ½ cup unsalted butter, softened

8 g / 1½ teaspoons fine sea salt

FOR THE EGG WASH

1 large egg yolk

Dash of milk or heavy cream

OPTIONAL TOPPING

1 tablespoon poppy or sesame seeds

MIX THE DOUGH

Place the warmed milk and honey in a large bowl and stir to combine. Sprinkle the yeast over the milk mixture and allow it to proof for about 10 minutes.

Add the sourdough starter and egg yolks to the bowl with the milk and stir into a slurry. Add the flours and mix with your hands until a thick, very sticky dough forms; scrape down the sides of the bowl and make sure to work the dough until all of the flour is well hydrated. Cover the bowl and allow the dough to autolyze at room temperature for about 20 minutes.

Sprinkle the salt evenly over the bowl and massage the softened butter into the dough. Continue working the dough in the bowl until the butter is evenly distributed and no streaks remain. The dough will be very tacky and will want to stick to your hands; this is natural. Avoid adding any additional flour to the dough. Remove the dough, clean and lightly oil your bowl, and then return the dough to the bowl. Cover and allow the dough to bulk proof in a warm location until it has at least doubled in size, about 2 hours.

SHAPE THE BUNS

Gently remove the dough from the bowl and place it on a lightly floured surface. Divide the dough into 12 even pieces (about 65 g each) and cover them with a towel.

To shape the buns, place one portion of dough onto an unfloured work surface. Cup your hand over the dough and move in a tight circular motion, letting your palm gently guide the top of the dough. When the dough is evenly round, transfer it to a parchment-lined sheet pan and continue forming the buns, spacing them about 2½ to 3 inches apart on the sheet pan. Cover the pan loosely with plastic and allow the buns to final proof in a warm location until they pass the poke test, about 1 hour.

BAKE

While the buns are proofing, preheat your oven to 350°F with a rack in the center position. When the buns are ready to bake, mix the egg yolk and cream in a small bowl and apply this wash to the tops of the buns using a pastry brush. Sprinkle the seeds (if using) evenly over the buns and bake in the center of the oven for about 20 minutes, rotating the pan halfway through baking. The buns are done when the tops are deep golden brown and a beautiful, buttery aroma wafts through the kitchen. Let the buns cool on a wire rack, and serve them warm or at room temperature.

TRY IT WITH . . . These buns need little to improve their flavor and texture, but if you must, try adorning them with some softened cultured butter or sweetened **Labneh**. **Kaya Jam** or a luscious fruit jam or marmalade would be appropriate, too. You may also slightly toast the buns on a grill for burgers with **Onion, Thyme, and Date Jam** and crumbled blue cheese. You could also use them for lamb sliders with **Labneh**, cucumber, and **Quickled** onions. If shaped into a loaf, this bread is excellent to use for **Baked Pain Perdu** . . . if you manage to have any leftovers, that is!

Chocolate & Orange Sourdough

— MAKES 1 LOAF —

This incredibly rich, heavy loaf is more of a dessert than a bread. The compounds resulting from the metabolic activities of a sourdough culture are responsible for the sour flavor that is particularly appreciated by many bread enthusiasts. For the same reasons that citrus can accentuate distinctive notes in chocolate, the complex acidic flavor compounds of sourdough can result in a similar taste sensation, accentuating the deep flavor profile of chocolate. This choice pairing results in a decadent loaf chock-full of dried fruit, nuts, and chocolate chunks, which is appropriately served during the holidays in lieu of fruitcake.

FOR THE SOAKER
75 g / ½ cup dried mission figs, chopped

20 g / 2 tablespoons Grand Marnier or Cointreau

½ teaspoon orange zest

FOR THE DOUGH
230 g / 1½ cups plus 2 tablespoons bread flour

55 g / ¼ cup medium rye flour

25 g / ¼ cup cocoa powder

90 g / scant ½ cup 100% hydration active sourdough starter, refreshed (page 10)

215 g / ¾ cup plus 5½ tablespoons water (75°F)

20 g / 1 tablespoon orange blossom honey

5 g / 1 teaspoon fine sea salt

55 g / ½ cup whole hazelnuts, toasted and coarsely chopped

45 g / ⅓ cup coarsely chopped bittersweet chocolate

MIX THE SOAKER
To prepare the soaker, mix together the figs, Grand Marnier, and orange zest in a small bowl. Cover the bowl and allow the mixture to steep at room temperature for 8 to 10 hours.

MIX THE DOUGH
Whisk together the flours and cocoa in a medium bowl until well combined. Set aside.

Place the active starter, water, and honey in a large bowl and stir to form a slurry. Slowly incorporate the flour mixture into the slurry, using your hands to mix until a shaggy dough forms with no dry lumps remaining. Cover the bowl and allow the dough to autolyze at room temperature for 20 to 30 minutes.

Sprinkle the salt over the dough and mix with your hands to distribute it evenly. Remove the dough from the bowl and perform a series of slap-and-folds on a clean surface for about 5 minutes.

Clean and lightly oil your large bowl and return the dough to it. Cover the bowl and allow the dough to rest at room temperature for 30 minutes.

Sprinkle the nuts, figs, and chocolate over the dough and fold it in to distribute. Cover the bowl again and bulk proof at room temperature until the dough has increased in size by at least one-third and feels springy and elastic to the touch, about 3½ hours, stretching and folding every 30 to 45 minutes.

SHAPE THE DOUGH

Remove the dough from the bowl and preshape it into a ball on a lightly floured work surface. Cover and allow it to relax for 10 to 30 minutes at room temperature.

Perform the final shaping, pulling and tucking the dough into the center to create a round form with surface tension. Pinch the seam closed and place the loaf in a well-floured proofing basket, seam-side up. Cover the basket with a cloth and then plastic, then place it in the refrigerator for 8 to 24 hours.

BAKE

Remove the loaf from the refrigerator and allow it to come to room temperature for about 1 hour. In the meantime, preheat a Dutch oven (preferably enamel coated) to 480°F for 20 minutes.

Sprinkle a touch of cornmeal on a piece of parchment paper cut to fit the bottom of the Dutch oven, and carefully flip your loaf onto it, seam-side down. Score the top of the loaf with a razor blade or lame, making a ¼- to ½-inch-deep slit down the center. Carefully lower the parchment and loaf into the preheated Dutch oven, position the lid, and return it to the oven.

Bake with the lid on for 20 minutes. Remove the lid and bake for another 12 to 20 minutes, tipping the loaf out of the pot and directly onto the oven rack after 6 to 10 minutes if your oven runs hot or if you are baking in non-enameled cast iron. The crust will be almost black (but not burnt) when done and will sound hollow when thumped on the bottom. Regardless of how tempting it may smell, allow the bread to cool completely before slicing in order for the crumb and the chocolate chunks to completely set.

TRY IT WITH . . . A little of this intensely flavored bread goes a long way with a touch of **Vanilla Marmalade**, **Cinnamon-Hazelnut Butter**, **Tahini Sauce**, or chèvre or another soft and slightly salty cheese. Although the keeping qualities of this loaf are excellent, you may want to double the batch and set one loaf out to go stale, using it to make a decadent serving of **Baked Pain Perdu**.

Sourdough
Whole-Grain Bagels

— MAKES 12 BAGELS —

For years I never understood the rage over bagels. Flat tasting with a dull, doughy texture, they never called to me from the corner delis in Brooklyn, and I smugly declined when they were brought to work meetings. Finally, a few naturally leavened bagels came my way with an increase in whole-grain flavor and a chewy, pleasant mouthfeel. The long-awaited bagel spell was finally cast and I now love preparing these an evening ahead of brunch with friends.

225 g / 1 cup plus 1 tablespoon 100% hydration
    active sourdough starter, refreshed (page 10)
340 g / 1½ cups water (70°F)
10 plus 85 g / ½ tablespoon plus ¼ cup
    barley malt syrup
330 g / 2⅓ cups bread flour
250 g / 2 cups plus 2½ tablespoons
    whole wheat flour
80 g / ¾ cup medium rye flour
10 g / 2 teaspoons fine sea salt

OPTIONAL TOPPINGS

These are beautiful baked plain or adorned with a combination of toppings. You can use ¼ cup of the following to dredge about 3 bagels: sesame, poppy, cumin, or flax seeds; flaked salt; Herb Salt; Old Bay seasoning; grated Parmesan cheese; and/or dried onion or garlic.

MIX THE DOUGH

In a large bowl, mix together the starter, water, and ½ tablespoon (10 g) of the barley malt syrup until a slurry forms. Add the flour and salt and mix in the bowl with your hands until the flour is incorporated. The dough will be stiff but workable. Cover the bowl and allow the dough to rest at room temperature for about 10 minutes.

Remove the dough from the bowl and knead it on a clean work surface for at least 10 minutes to develop dough strength, taking short breaks if needed. Clean and lightly grease the bowl and return the dough, rolling it in the oil to coat. Cover the bowl with plastic and allow the dough to bulk ferment at room temperature until it is puffy and almost doubled in size, about 4 hours, turning and folding at least once.

SHAPE THE DOUGH

Remove the dough from the bowl and divide it into 12 equal pieces. Pat each piece into a roughly 5 × 12-inch rectangle.

Fold each rectangle from the top down, tightly tucking each successive fold into the next. With your hands, roll the dough piece into a long, 10-inch coil, slightly tapered at the ends. Shape the coil into a donut with a roughly 2-inch-diameter hole in the center, overlapping the ends to seal the circle. With your index and middle fingers inserted through the hole, roll the bagel where the ends are overlapped to reinforce the seal.

Place the bagels on a sheet pan with about 2 inches of space between each bagel. Allow them to proof at room temperature until they are visibly swollen and pass the poke test, 45 minutes to 1 hour. Cover the sheet pan with a towel and then plastic and place it in the refrigerator for 8 to 12 hours or overnight.

BOIL AND BAKE

Remove the bagels from the fridge and allow them to come to room temperature for about 1 hour, or longer if your room is held below 70°F. Meanwhile, preheat the oven to 500°F.

Prepare the water bath by stirring together 85 g (¼ cup) of barley malt syrup and 4 to 5 quarts of water in a large stock pot over high heat. Bring to a rolling boil and carefully drop the proofed bagels in the water bath 4 to 5 at a time, depending on the size of your pot. (Do not crowd the bagels.) Boil for about 30 seconds on each side, then use a slotted spoon to transfer the bagels to a wire rack to drain. Repeat with the remaining uncooked bagels and let them cool for a few minutes on the wire rack before handling. Roll each boiled bagel in seeds (if using), and place them on parchment-lined sheet pans with about 1½ to 2 inches of space between each bagel.

Bake the bagels for about 15 minutes, rotating the sheet pans halfway, until the bagels are golden brown. Remove them from the oven and let them rest on a wire rack until they are cool enough to handle; serve immediately. These are best eaten the same day but will freeze beautifully or toast well for up to 2 days.

TRY IT WITH . . . For a bagel brunch full of luscious sweet jams and savory flavors, have a quality cream cheese on the ready and a platter of **Beet-Cured Gravlax** to impress your guests. Pile a pickle plate high with **Fermented Pickles**, **Kraut**, and/or **Quickles**. **Baccalà Mantecato** is also excellent served with **Horseradish Apple Cream**, shaved fennel, and a sprinkling of fresh herbs or arugula. For a nondairy alternative, try the **Crema de Carciofi**, too. Sweet spreads such as **Blushing Goat Spread** are appropriate as well as soft butter and any assortment of jams. These make a fine choice for an **Egg Salad** sandwich.

Spelt English Muffins

— MAKES 5 TO 6 MUFFINS —

These whole-grain muffins have a tender, almost sweet aroma and are a wonderful alternative to those made with mostly refined flour. Their crumb structure may not be nearly as craggy as what you are used to in a commercially prepared English muffin, but their flavor will make the trade-off barely noticeable! If you wish to make a large batch to freeze, simply double this recipe. Otherwise, these are best eaten straight off the griddle. For a lighter muffin, substitute the whole spelt flour for an equal weight of sifted spelt flour or all-purpose flour. You may also substitute whole-milk yogurt. (Recipe shown on page 138.)

---

75 g / ¼ cup plus 1 tablespoon buttermilk
   (100°F)

15 g / 2¼ teaspoons mild honey

¼ teaspoon active dry yeast (optional)

125 g / ½ cup plus 1 tablespoon 100% hydration
   active sourdough starter, refreshed (page 10)

165 g / 1½ cups whole spelt flour

3 g / ½ teaspoon fine sea salt

15 g / 1 tablespoon unsalted butter

Place the warm buttermilk and honey in a medium bowl and stir to combine. Sprinkle the yeast (if using) over the mixture, and allow it to proof for a few minutes. Add the sourdough starter, flour, and salt and mix with your hands until a sticky dough forms and no lumps remain. Cover the bowl and let the dough proof at room temperature until it is puffy, about 1 hour. Alternatively, if you are using sourdough leavening only, cover the bowl and bulk proof for about 2 to 2½ hours, until the dough visually increases in size by one-third.

Remove the dough from the bowl and place it on a lightly floured work surface. With a rolling pin or the palm of your hand, form the dough into an even circle about 1½ inches thick. Using a 2½- to 3-inch biscuit cutter, cut out 5 to 6 circles, rerolling the dough if necessary.

Line a sheet pan with parchment paper and lightly dust the parchment with cornmeal or semolina. Place the circles on the parchment, cover the pan, and allow the circles to proof until at least doubled in thickness, about 1 to 1½ hours if using baker's yeast, 2 to 2½ hours if not.

Place a large skillet with a lid over low heat for about 3 minutes. Add the butter, swirling to coat, and arrange the muffins in the pan, being careful not to crowd them too close. Cook for 5 to 6 minutes with the lid on, until the muffins have a nice brown ring on the bottom and have visibly lifted in the pan. Flip and cook the other sides for another 5 to 6 minutes, checking the bottoms in the last few minutes of cooking. If they seem to be browning too fast, simply turn off the heat and let them finish cooking in the hot pan. Remove the muffins from the pan and let them cool enough to handle on a wire rack before serving.

TRY IT WITH . . . Using a fork, split the muffins around their circumferences to get the characteristic craggy crumb. You may then choose to toast them before slathering with butter and a jam of your choice. These also make a wonderful brunch canvas for **Spring Medley**, **Warm Brussels Sprouts Salad** or **Sorghum-Roasted Carrots**, and a poached egg.

Soft Pretzels & Pretzel Rolls

— MAKES 16 SMALL, APPETIZER-SIZE PRETZELS; 8 HAPPY HOUR–SIZE PRETZELS;
OR 8 PRETZEL BUNS —

Traditional Bavarian pretzels are a treat to behold, especially when accompanied by a hefty stein of beer. The key to their characteristic dark, chewy skin is dipping them into a caustic lye solution before baking. To make the process more accessible to the home baker, however, an alkaline solution is created by using baking soda instead. This solution acts to break down the proteins in the crust, balancing the sugars and amino acids in the heat-activated Maillard Reaction responsible for the pretzels' brown appearance.

This recipe makes two pretzel sizes or a small bun, the smaller of which is easier to handle when dropping them into and taking them out of the hot bath. If you choose to make the larger pretzel, make sure you have a large slotted spoon that will accommodate their size. This is also an excellent dough for making pretzel buns (see Kitchen Note).

115 g / ½ cup water (100°F)
20 g / 1 tablespoon mild honey
1 teaspoon active dry yeast, optional
170 g / ¾ cup 100% hydration active sourdough
    starter, refreshed (page 10)
490 g / 3½ cups bread flour
70 g / ⅔ cup whole rye flour

10 g / 2 teaspoons fine sea salt
20 g / 1 tablespoon barley malt syrup
55 g / ¼ cup baking soda

FOR THE GARNISH
15 g / 1 tablespoon Herb Salt or coarse salt

MIX THE DOUGH

Place 115 g (½ cup) of the warm water in a large bowl and stir in the honey. Sprinkle the yeast (if using) over the mixture, and allow it to proof for about 10 minutes.

Stir in an additional ¾ cup (170 g) of warm water and the sourdough starter until a slurry forms. Slowly add the flour and mix with your hands to form a shaggy, somewhat stiff mass. Cover the bowl and allow the dough to autolyze at room temperature for about 20 minutes.

Add the salt and work it into the dough with your hands. Remove the dough from the bowl and knead it on a clean work surface for about 5 minutes. This helps to develop the strength of the dough, ensuring that the pretzels will be light but chewy. If the dough feels resistant or begins to tear, simply set it aside, cover it with a towel, and allow it to relax for a few minutes before resuming kneading. Clean and lightly oil the bowl before returning the dough to it. Cover the bowl and allow the dough to bulk proof in a warm location until it has doubled in size, about 2 hours. If developing the dough without the additional yeast, let it bulk proof at room temperature for about 3 hours or until it has increased in size by about one-third.

SHAPE THE DOUGH

Line 2 sheet pans with parchment paper and lightly oil the parchment. Remove the dough from the bowl and deflate it on a lightly floured surface. Divide the dough into 16 equal-size pieces (about 60 g each), or 8 pieces (about 120 g each) if making the larger pretzels. Cover the dough loosely with plastic while you work.

On a clean surface, roll each piece of dough into a coil about 12 to 14 inches long for the smaller size and 16 to 18 inches long for the larger pretzels, tapering the ends as you work.

To form the pretzel shape, hold one end of the coil in each hand and cross the two ends twice to create a twist. Lay the twist over the looped side of the coil and press gently to adhere. Place the formed pretzel on one of the prepared sheet pans and repeat, leaving about 3 inches between each pretzel. Cover the pans loosely and allow them to final proof for about 20 minutes. If using dough without the added yeast, cover the pans with a towel and then plastic and allow the pretzels to retard in the refrigerator overnight. Remove from the refrigerator approximately 1 hour before boiling and baking.

BOIL AND BAKE

Preheat your oven to 425°F. Place two cooling racks over a dry towel on your work surface. While the pretzels are final proofing, bring 10 to 12 cups of water to a boil in a very deep pot and stir in the barley malt syrup. Carefully add the baking soda to the boiling water. (This will cause the water to foam tremendously, so be prepared to react accordingly, avoiding unnecessary burns by quickly removing your hands from danger.) Gently drop a pretzel into the alkaline bath and check to see if it floats. If not, discard and continue to proof the rest of the pretzels for another 5 to 7 minutes, until ready. Boil 4 small or 2 large pretzels at a time for no more than 30 seconds on each side. Remove the boiled pretzels from the bath and allow them to drain on the prepared cooling racks while you boil the rest of the pretzels.

When all the pretzels have been boiled and drained, transfer them to the previously lined sheet pans and sprinkle with coarse salt. Bake for about 14 minutes for the smaller pretzels or 5 to 7 minutes longer for the larger pretzels, until they are deep golden brown. Remove the pretzels from the oven and allow them to cool on wire racks. Serve them warm or at room temperature. These are best enjoyed the same day they are baked.

TRY IT WITH . . . Although not traditionally Bavarian, soft pretzels are excellent served with **Fermented Grainy Mustard** or soft salted butter. The hearty, chewy nature of pretzel rolls is excellent for serving **Egg Salad**, or grilled sausages or smoked duck breast with **Fermented Grainy Mustard** and/or **Homemade Mayonnaise**, **Kraut**, and spicy nasturtium or mustard leaves.

KITCHEN NOTE This dough can easily be formed into rolls instead of pretzels. For sandwich-size rolls, divide the dough into eight 120-gram pieces. Follow the shaping instructions for the Oat Flour Brioche on page 65 if making round buns, or follow the instructions for Pain de Mie on page 57 if making oblong buns, tucking under the ends. Once the buns have proofed, simply boil them for 1 minute before draining, scoring as you wish, and salting. Bake in a 425°F oven for about 20 minutes or until a deep golden color is achieved.

If your pretzels or buns take on an overly wrinkled appearance after baking, this is most likely because they sat too long in the hot water bath.

2

Crackers, Cakes & Scones

Wʜᴇɴ ʏᴏᴜ'ʀᴇ in the mood to turn on the oven and bake something uniquely delicious and satisfying without the time commitment of a loaf of bread, this chapter provides plenty of recipes to satisfy your cravings. From flavorful crackers, to buttery prefermented Drop Biscuits, to a rich and wholesome Olive Oil Cake or boozy scones, there is a little something for every occasion.

◄ *Left to right*: Currant Cream Scones; Blackberry, Apple, and Sage Jam; Olive Oil Cake (chocolate, rosemary, pine nut, and cacao nib variation); Drop Biscuits; Crème Fraîche (clotted cream variation).

Lavash

— MAKES 6 FLATBREADS —

Bread making is a practice as old as civilization and whose methods reflect the cultural expressions of the time and place in which they were created. Using a humble set of ingredients, bread is made with reverence in many countries where its alchemy is respected and where it is an important source of calories for many people. In developing this recipe, I held a heavy heart for the millions of families who have been displaced from their homes by war, separated from their traditional hearths, and denied the most basic source of life we so often take for granted.

Flatbreads are an ancient food made in different iterations by the people of North Africa, the Middle East, and Central Asia—cultures that use an open-fire heat source or a barrel-type oven quite different from what is present in most conventional Western homes. This lavash, a leavened bread of Turkey, Georgia, Armenia, Azerbaijan, Syria, and Iran, is easily adapted using a hearthstone placed on the middle rack of your oven. If you want to enjoy its soft, pliable nature, it is best served warm, fresh from the oven. Since these thin breads dry out quickly, they can also be enjoyed as crackers or sprinkled with water and wrapped in a towel to rehydrate. For this reason, they make an excellent transportable food for nomadic peoples. (Recipe shown on page 176.)

---

115 g / ½ cup water (100°F)

10 g / ½ tablespoon mild honey

Small pinch of active dry yeast (optional)

100 g / ½ cup 100% hydration active sourdough
    starter, refreshed (page 10)

175 g / 1¼ cups bread flour

65 g / ½ cup Type T-85 wheat flour
    (high-extraction bread flour)

5 g / ½ teaspoon fine sea salt

MIX THE DOUGH

Mix the warm water and honey together in a medium bowl. Sprinkle in the yeast (if using), and allow it to proof for about 10 minutes.

Stir in the starter until a slurry forms. Add the flours to the bowl and mix with your hands until you have a shaggy mass. Cover the bowl and allow the dough to autolyze at room temperature for about 20 minutes.

Remove the dough from the bowl and place it on a generously floured surface. Sprinkle the salt evenly over the dough and knead the dough until the salt is fully incorporated, about 5 minutes. If the dough seems sticky, dust your work surface with a little more flour, continuing to knead until the dough feels soft and supple. Clean and lightly oil your bowl, then return the dough to it. Cover the bowl and allow the dough to bulk proof at room temperature until at least doubled in size, about 2 to 2½ hours, or 3½ hours if you omitted the commercial yeast. About 30 to 45 minutes before you feel the dough is ready, preheat a hearthstone on the middle rack of your oven to 500°F.

SHAPE THE FLATBREADS

Remove the dough from the bowl and divide it into 6 equal-size pieces; cover them lightly with a damp towel. Using a rolling pin, roll out 2 pieces at a time. When you feel the dough pieces resist, simply set them aside, cover, and allow them to relax into their new shape. Continue working the remaining dough, alternating between flatbreads until they reach a nice uneven shape, about 8 to 10 inches long. The thinner you roll the breads, the more they will dry out and become cracker-like. Alternatively, if you roll them a bit thicker, about ⅛ to ¼ inch, they will puff up and be a bit more pillowy when baked, similar to a pita bread.

BAKE

Using a lightly floured peel or the back of a sheet pan lined with parchment paper, carefully place the flatbreads onto the hearthstone, one at a time, avoiding wrinkles or folds. Bake for about 2 to 3 minutes, flip, and continue to bake for another 2 to 3 minutes. Repeat until all the breads are baked. Serve warm for softer bread or as crackers the next day. Lavash will keep for weeks wrapped in paper at room temperature, served as crackers.

TRY IT WITH . . . These versatile flatbreads are excellent stuffed with any manner of savory fillings, including **Preserved Lemon and Fava Bean Hummus**, roasted or sautéed vegetables of your choice, or **Pan-Fried Cauliflower in Curried Yogurt Marinade** drizzled with **Tahini Sauce**.

Dipping Chips

— SERVES 4 —

This is an excellent way to use up leftover flatbreads, transforming them into savory crisps for dipping. If you do not have Dukkah prepared (page 184), you may use zaatar spice or sesame seeds instead. (Recipe shown on page 166.)

---

160 g / 3 Lavash (page 80), cut or broken
    into small wedges
3 tablespoons extra-virgin olive oil
1 plump garlic clove, minced

1½ tablespoons Dukkah (page 184)
¾ teaspoon Citrus Salt or Herb Salt
    (pages 183 and 182)

Preheat the oven to 350°F.

    Place the lavash pieces in a large bowl. In a small bowl, whisk together the olive oil, garlic, Dukkah, and Citrus Salt or Herb Salt. Drizzle the mixture evenly over the flatbread pieces and gently toss until well coated.

    Spread the coated pieces of lavash on a lined sheet pan in a single layer and transfer to the oven. Bake for 10 to 12 minutes, stirring halfway through. Check on the chips in the last 3 to 4 minutes of baking and remove them from the oven when they are toasty brown in color. Store in a paper bag and serve within a week of baking.

TRY IT WITH . . . These are excellent served with **Preserved Lemon and Fava Bean Hummus**; **Egg Salad**; **Spicy Cheddar, Almond, and Olive Ball**; or **Crema de Carciofi**.

Seeded Seaweed
Snacking Crisps

— SERVES 6 TO 8 —

These naturally gluten-free, vegan snacking crisps are packed with texture and make a wonderful canvas for savory spreads. Although you can flavor them as you wish, I like to be generous with togarashi and garlic. Full of omega-3s, protein, fiber, and healthy fats, these are sure to provide a boost of late-afternoon energy, helping you to power through the workday. They are also versatile served as cocktail appetizers.

If your body has trouble digesting seeds, soak them before using to help eliminate phytic acid compounds.

70 g / ½ cup sunflower seeds or pepitas

90 g / ½ cup chia seeds

60 g / ½ cup whole flax seeds

65 g / ½ cup sesame seed flour

10 g / ½ cup arame seaweed

15 g / 3 teaspoons ground togarashi

5 g / 1 teaspoon fine sea salt

½ teaspoon orange zest

1 plump garlic clove (8 g), grated

210 g / ¾ cup plus 4 tablespoons water (100°F)

20 g / 1½ tablespoons toasted sesame oil

10 g / 2 teaspoons tamari

10 g / ½ tablespoon mild honey

Whisk together the dry ingredients, zest, and garlic in a large bowl. Drizzle in the warm water, oil, tamari, and honey. Mix thoroughly with a spoon or your hands to form a paste, then cover the bowl with plastic and let it stand at room temperature for at least 20 minutes or up to 1 day, depending on your digestive preference.

Preheat your oven to 350°F and line a sheet pan with parchment paper. With wet hands, press the congealed dough into the prepared pan, creating a thin, even layer. The mixture may initially feel dry, but it will come together to just fill the pan.

Bake for 25 minutes, rotating the pan halfway through. Remove the pan from the oven and slice the crackers into serving sizes using a pizza wheel or chef's knife. Flip the crackers over and bake for another 25 minutes. They are done when the edges are a warm brown color and the sunflower seeds are a toasty golden color. Remove the crackers from the oven and let them cool completely on a wire rack before serving. Store in a paper bag at room temperature for up to 1 week.

TRY IT WITH . . . Spread with a dollop of **Labneh** or **Lemony Herb Chèvre**, or dip into **Preserved Lemon and Fava Bean Hummus**, and top with microgreens, sliced radishes, **Rainbow Relish**, **Roasted Cherry Tomato Confit**, or even a little jam to satisfy that sweet craving. The bold citrus flavors of **Vanilla Marmalade** or **Tomato Marmalade** or even **Watermelon Jelly** blend beautifully with the spicy umami flavors of these crackers.

Sourdough Rye Crackers

— MAKES 1 DOZEN 3- TO 4-INCH CRACKERS —

These crackers are a cinch to prepare and can be made ahead for entertaining or to have on hand as snack food. The seeds and flavorings are adaptable, so if you don't care for caraway, simply omit it and substitute with your favorite spice, such as cumin, nigella seeds, or ground fenugreek. (Recipe shown on page 118.)

250 g / 1¼ cup 100% hydration active sourdough starter, refreshed (page 10)
60 g / ¼ cup plus 1 teaspoon extra-virgin olive oil
160 g / 1 cup whole rye flour
5 g / 1 teaspoon fine sea salt
2 teaspoons sesame seeds
1 teaspoon poppy seeds

1 teaspoon caraway seeds
1 teaspoon dried onion (optional)
1 teaspoon dried garlic (optional)

FOR THE TOPPING
Light sprinkle of flaked sea salt (optional)

In a medium bowl, mix together the starter and oil. Stir in the flour, salt, seeds, and spices (if using) and mix with your hands until a shaggy mass forms. Remove the dough from the bowl and knead it on a lightly floured work surface for about 1 minute or until a smooth, even mass forms, adding flour if necessary. Clean the bowl and return the dough. Cover the bowl and allow the dough to rest for at least 30 minutes or up to 2 hours for improved flavor.

Preheat the oven to 425°F. Turn the dough out onto a lightly floured work surface and divide it into 2 even pieces. Wrap one piece in plastic and set it aside while you roll out the other to a ¼- to ⅛-inch thickness. The thinner the cracker, the lighter and crispier it will be. Sprinkle the flaked sea salt (if using) over the top and gently press it into the surface.

Using a pastry wheel, cut the crackers into 3- to 4-inch rectangles and transfer them to a parchment-lined sheet pan. (Alternatively, you may use a cookie cutter for themed shapes, rerolling if necessary to use up all of the dough.) With a watchful eye, bake for 9 to 12 minutes, depending on the thickness and size of the crackers. They are done when the edges turn golden brown. Remove the crackers from the oven and let them cool on a wire rack while you repeat the process with the second half of the dough. These will keep well for up to 2 weeks stored in a paper bag at room temperature.

TRY IT WITH . . . Savory but versatile, these crackers can be served with a variety of dips or sweet toppings. I especially love them with **Lemony Herb Chèvre**; **Blue Cheese Spread**; **Spicy Cheddar, Almond, and Olive Ball**; **Vanilla Marmalade**; or **Violet Petal Jam**; or dipped into **Preserved Lemon and Fava Bean Hummus** and served with **S'chug**.

Garlic Crostini

These are easy to prepare ahead of time and are an excellent way to bring a stale loaf of bread to life. You may use any type of bread cut into small, appetizer-size pieces, but A Modest Baguette (page 53) or Moonbread (page 50) makes for perfect crostini. (Recipe shown on page 158.)

---

1 baguette or tordu, sliced into ½-inch-thick pieces

6 garlic cloves (40 g), peeled and sliced in half

110 g / ½ cup extra-virgin olive oil

1 teaspoon flaked sea salt

Generously and vigorously rub both sides of each piece of bread with the cut sides of the garlic halves. Brush a moderate coating of olive oil onto each side and lightly sprinkle with flaked sea salt.

Preheat a grill or grill pan to medium-low and toast the bread slices until grill marks appear on the bottom. Flip and repeat. Alternatively, you may place the pieces onto a sheet pan and toast under the broiler, carefully checking and flipping after 2 to 3 minutes or when color appears. Continue to toast until both sides are light brown and crisp. Serve warm or at room temperature.

TRY IT WITH . . . The toasted nature of crostini gives them the structural fortitude to be used for either dipping, spreading, or topping. They are versatile and excellent with a variety of recipes, from **Blue Cheese Spread**, **Crema de Carciofi**, and **Preserved Lemon and Fava Bean Hummus**, to the **Spicy Cheddar, Almond, and Olive Ball** or even **Onion, Thyme, and Date Jam**. For entertaining, you may wish to provide a few of these choices on a platter along with playful garnishes, such as thinly sliced radishes and fresh herbs.

Olive Oil Cake

— MAKES 1 LOAF —

Olive oil imparts a moist, almost savory crumb to balance the mild sweetness of this adaptable recipe. If you prefer a more pronounced, fruit-forward flavor, use a good-quality extra-virgin olive oil. You may choose to omit the spice variations for a more neutral backdrop, but I love to play with the pairings in making small finger sandwiches.

Juniper berries are the fruit of *Juniperus virginiana*, the tree commonly known as Eastern red cedar. These berries are used to flavor gin as well as the French liqueur Chartreuse. Whether you use freshly harvested juniper berries or dried and ground berries in this cake, they will impart a spicy, aromatic quality that blends beautifully with cinnamon, nutmeg, and allspice. (Chocolate variation shown on page 78.)

---

115 g / ¾ cup all-purpose flour

80 g / ½ cup whole spelt flour

1 teaspoon baking powder

½ teaspoon baking soda

½ teaspoon fine sea salt

200 g / 1 cup granulated sugar

5 g / 1½ teaspoons orange zest

2 large eggs (100 g)

205 g / ¾ cup plain whole-milk yogurt

100 g / ½ cup olive oil

FOR COFFEE, BLACK PEPPER, AND CARDAMOM VARIATION

1½ tablespoon ground coffee

2 teaspoons ground cardamom

1 teaspoon black pepper

FOR CHOCOLATE, ROSEMARY, PINE NUT, AND CACAO NIB VARIATION

Substitute ½ cup (50 g) dark cocoa powder
    for ¼ cup (40 g) of the spelt flour

1 tablespoon minced fresh rosemary

1 teaspoon vanilla extract

50 g / ⅓ cup pine nuts, toasted

35 g / ⅓ cup cacao nibs

FOR JUNIPER SPICE VARIATION

1 teaspoon juniper berries, ground with
    a mortar and pestle

½ teaspoon ground allspice berries

½ teaspoon ground cinnamon

¼ teaspoon ground nutmeg

Preheat your oven to 325°F and generously grease and flour a loaf tin.

In a small bowl, whisk together the flour, baking powder and soda, salt, and spices (from your desired variation). Set aside.

In a separate large bowl, smoosh together the sugar and zest with the back of a spoon to release the fragrant citrus oils. Add the eggs and beat with a spoon or a hand mixer until ribbons fall from the spoon or beater when lifted. Add the yogurt and olive oil and beat to combine.

Fold the flour mixture into the liquid mixture, one-third at a time, stirring to combine and being careful not to over mix. Pour the batter into the prepared tin and bake for 55 to 60 minutes or until a toothpick inserted into the center of the cake comes out clean. Remove the cake from the oven and allow it to rest for 5 to 7 minutes, then turn it out onto a wire rack to cool.

TRY IT WITH . . . When sliced, this cake makes excellent tea sandwiches layered with a thick dollop of homemade **Crème Fraîche** or a smear of **Labneh**, followed by your choice of rich fruit topping. **Caramel Apple Bourbon Butter** and **Spiced Concord Grape Jam** marry well with any of these spice variations.

Pistachio Cardamom Crumb Muffins

These moderately sweet muffins are soft and warmly spiced, with a crunchy crumb topping laced with pistachios. They are a lovely treat for a weekend morning, when they make the whole house smell like a warm cup of chai.

FOR THE STREUSEL

55 g / ½ cup whole wheat pastry flour

100 g / ¾ cup raw, shelled pistachios, coarsely chopped

105 g / ½ cup packed light brown sugar

1 teaspoon ground cardamom

¼ teaspoon ground cinnamon

¼ teaspoon ground allspice

Pinch of salt

75 g / 5 tablespoons unsalted butter

FOR THE MUFFINS

110 g / 1 cup whole wheat pastry flour

120 g / 1 cup all-purpose flour

2 teaspoons baking powder

1 teaspoon ground cardamom

½ teaspoon ground allspice

½ teaspoon ground cinnamon

½ teaspoon ground ginger

½ teaspoon fine sea salt

115 g / ½ cup unsalted butter, softened

70 g / ¼ cup packed light brown sugar

½ teaspoon lemon zest

2 large eggs (100 g)

½ teaspoon vanilla extract

175 g / ¾ cup whole milk

MAKE THE STREUSEL

Preheat your oven to 375°F and generously grease and flour a muffin tin.

Whisk together the flour, pistachios, sugar, spices, and salt in a medium bowl. Cut in the butter and massage with your fingers until the mixture resembles pea-size crumbs. Cover and refrigerate until ready to use.

MIX THE BATTER

In a medium bowl, whisk together the flours, baking powder, spices, and salt. Set aside.

In a separate large bowl, beat together the butter, sugar, and lemon zest with a hand-held mixer until light and fluffy. Add the eggs one at a time and beat until the mixture is thick and creamy. Beat in the vanilla. Add the flour mixture and milk to the egg mixture, alternating between additions. Stir gently, being careful not to overmix, until the batter is relatively smooth.

BAKE
Spoon the batter into the cups of the prepared muffin tin, filling each cup about half to three-quarters full. Finish with the chilled streusel topping. Place the muffin tin on a sheet pan and bake for 22 to 24 minutes or until a toothpick inserted into the center of a muffin comes out clean. Remove the muffins from the oven and allow them to sit for 3 to 4 minutes before turning them out onto a wire rack to cool. These are best served warm or at room temperature the day they are baked.

TRY IT WITH . . . Already heavily spiced but only moderately sweet, these delectable whole-grain muffins pair well with **Rose-Scented Labneh**, **Strawberry and Meyer Lemon Preserves**, **Vanilla Marmalade**, and **Prickly Pear and Aperol Jelly**.

Currant Cream Scones

— MAKES 6 SMALL OR 4 LARGE SCONES —

Scones are a wonderful canvas for a number of different jams, curds, and creams, and they make a perfect accompaniment to afternoon tea. Feel free to omit the currants if you desire a more neutral, slightly sweet scone, or substitute the currants with cranberries and orange zest instead. As an alternative to the Grand Marnier, you may soak the currants in wine or port before folding them into the dough. Homemade Crème Fraîche (page 208) makes these amazingly tender and moist, but sour cream will work just as well.

FOR THE SOAKER
80 g / ½ cup dried currants
30 g / 3 tablespoons Grand Marnier or
    Cointreau

FOR THE EGG WASH
1 large egg yolk
Generous dash of heavy cream
1 to 2 tablespoons coarse sugar

FOR THE DOUGH
120 g / 1 cup all-purpose flour
110 g / 1 cup whole wheat pastry flour
65 g / ⅓ cup granulated sugar
2 teaspoons baking powder
½ teaspoon fine sea salt
70 g / 5 tablespoons cold unsalted butter, cubed
45 g / 3 tablespoons Crème Fraîche (page 208)
20 to 30 g / 2 to 3 tablespoons whole milk
1 large egg (50 g)
1 teaspoon lemon zest
10 g / 1 tablespoon freshly squeezed lemon juice

At least 2 hours before you plan to make the scones (or even better, the night before), make the soaker. Stir together the currants and liqueur in a small bowl, cover with with plastic or a clean towel, and set aside to soak at room temperature.

Preheat the oven to 400°F and line a sheet pan with parchment paper.

To make the dough, whisk together the flour, sugar, baking powder, and salt in a large bowl. Working quickly, cut in the butter with your fingers or a pastry blender until the mixture resembles coarse meal. (Alternatively, you may perform this step in a food processor.)

In a separate small bowl, whisk together the crème fraîche, 2 tablespoons of the whole milk, the egg, lemon zest, and lemon juice. Stir in the currants and then fold this mixture into the flour and butter mixture until the dough just starts to come together, using a light hand as you would making biscuits—do not overmix. If the mixture feels dry, add another tablespoon of milk and mix just until it binds together.

To make the egg wash, whisk together the egg yolk and cream.

Remove the dough from the bowl and place it on a lightly floured work surface. Pat or roll the dough into a slab about ¾ to 1 inch thick. Using a bench knife or biscuit cutter, cut out 6 small scones or divide the dough into 4 larger scones, gently rerolling the dough if necessary. Place the scones on the prepared sheet pan and brush the tops of the scones with the egg wash. Sprinkle generously with coarse sugar and bake for about 15 to 17 minutes or until the tops are golden. Remove the scones from the oven and let them cool slightly on a wire rack; serve warm.

TRY IT WITH . . . These are delicious served with **Clotted Cream**, **Violet Petal Jam**, **Prickly Pear and Aperol Jelly**, **Vanilla Marmalade**, **Strawberry and Meyer Lemon Preserves**, or really any jam or jelly you prefer!

KITCHEN NOTE Cold scones or biscuits that go into a hot oven have a better rise and tenderer crumb. If your kitchen is a bit warm while mixing, try popping the formed scones into the freezer for 10 to 15 minutes before baking.

Drop Biscuits

— MAKES 12 SMALL BISCUITS —

This recipe uses a fermented soaking method to prepare the rather coarse graham flour, both tenderizing the grain and making it more digestible. The result is an incredibly rich and buttery whole-grain biscuit with a creamy, nut-like flavor. Be sure to source a quality, freshly milled graham flour to presoak, and whip these up in minutes for a quick brunch or afternoon tea, or to serve with a Southern-style dinner. There is no rolling or cutting out of the biscuits, so the chance for them to be tough from overworking is minimized!

150 g / 1 cup graham flour

220 g / 1 cup plain whole-milk yogurt

120 g / 1 cup all-purpose flour

10 g / 2 teaspoons baking powder

5 g / 1 teaspoon fine sea salt

115 g / ½ cup cold unsalted butter, cut into chunks

Stir together the graham flour and yogurt in a small bowl, cover, and refrigerate for 6 to 8 hours or up to 24 hours.

When you are ready to make the biscuits, preheat your oven to 400°F and line a sheet pan with parchment paper.

In a medium bowl, whisk together the all-purpose flour, baking powder, and salt. Add the cold butter chunks and, working quickly, use your fingers or a pastry blender to cut in the butter until the flour resembles coarse meal. (Alternatively, you may perform this step in a food processor.)

With a fork, lightly stir in the graham-yogurt mixture until lightly incorporated. Using an ice cream scoop or your hands, drop small walnut-size balls of dough onto the prepared sheet pan. Bake for 20 to 22 minutes or until the tops of the biscuits are golden and the bottoms are a warm brown. Serve warm.

TRY IT WITH . . . When you grow up Southern, there's really never a time when biscuits aren't welcome at the table! They have so much flavor that they need little else, but try melting a little butter into the middle while still warm and serve with **Caramel Apple Bourbon Butter**, **Gingered Sweet Potato Butter**, or really any fruit jam of your choosing. These also make delicious strawberry shortcakes topped with fresh strawberries, **Strawberry and Meyer Lemon Preserves** or **Honey-Roasted Rhubarb Compote**, and whipped or **Clotted Cream** and a drizzle of honey.

Baked Pain Perdu

— MAKES 6 SERVINGS —

Although I love French toast, I dread the tedious boredom of standing over a griddle wait-ing for the slices to brown while a crowd of hungry guests waits impatiently, salivating at the table. This recipe makes use of otherwise "lost bread," soaked in a custard mixture the night before, making breakfast or brunch as easy as sliding the pan into the oven and baking until golden, puffed, and ready for your favorite topping. For best results, use a crusty hearth loaf of rather stale bread, allowing it to generously soak up the eggs, milk, and butter. If it is a fresh loaf or an enriched bread such as Pain de Mie (page 57) or Buckwheat Milk Bread (page 61), slice thickly and spread the pieces out to dry the day before you intend to do the soak. Softer breads will soak up the custard in about an hour rather than the overnight treatment that crusty and stale hearth loaves require.

---

795 g / 1¾ pounds stale bread, sliced into
    1¼-inch-thick pieces
460 g / 2 cups whole milk (or nut milk of your
    choosing), room temperature
55 g / ¼ cup unsalted butter, melted and cooled
6 large eggs (300 g), room temperature

4 g / 2 tablespoons mild honey
3 g / 1 teaspoon vanilla extract
3 g / 1 teaspoon orange zest
¼ teaspoon fine sea salt
15 g / 1 tablespoon coarse sugar
¼ teaspoon ground cinnamon

Layer the pieces of stale crusty bread in a large buttered roasting pan, overlapping them somewhat like fallen dominoes.

In a medium bowl, whisk together the milk, butter, eggs, honey, vanilla, orange zest, and salt. Pour this mixture evenly over the bread, carefully flipping the pieces to encourage contact between the bread and the custard mixture. Cover the pan and allow it to soak in the refrigerator overnight.

The next day, remove the pan from the refrigerator and bring it to room temperature. Line and generously butter a large sheet pan and preheat your oven to 425°F. Arrange the pieces of soaked bread on the pan, lying them flat without overlapping. Whisk together the sugar and cinnamon and sprinkle this mixture over the toast. Bake until the bread is golden, about 25 to 30 minutes.

TRY IT WITH . . . Warmed maple syrup or chilled **Kaya Jam** is an excellent choice, but any manner of fruit topping is appropriate as well, including **Honey-Roasted Rhubarb Compote**.

PART TWO

JAM

3

Jam

"When spring came, even the false spring, there were no problems except where to be the happiest."

—ERNEST HEMINGWAY, *A Moveable Feast*

THE FOLLOWING RECIPES provide suggestions for the best way to capture sunshine in a jar. Whether it be the first rays of spring made into a brilliant, purple Violet Petal Jam (page 103) or the sweet, almost custard-like, drizzly texture of coconut bottled into Kaya Jam (page 143) during winter, each season is well represented with ingredients meant to inspire you in the kitchen and lure you into the orchard or wild garden.

◀ *On spoons, left to right*: Peach and Tea Preserves (apricot variation); Strawberry and Meyer Lemon Preserves; Cherry, Apple, and Almond Conserve; Dandelion and Turmeric Jelly. *Bottom right*: Violet Petal Jam. *In jars, left to right*: Peach and Tea Preserves (apricot variation), Dandelion and Turmeric Jelly. *Also shown*: skillet-toasted Miche.

Violet Petal Jam

— MAKES 5 CUPS OR 2½ PINTS —

It takes a bit of time to collect and clean enough violets to make jam. Solicit the help of a lover or close friend so you can enjoy the long-awaited rays of spring sunshine warming your faces as you work and engage in leisurely conversation. Look for wild violet flowers on leafless stalks surrounded by deep green, heart-shaped leaves fairly low to the ground. They grow naturally in woodlands, thickets, and stream banks and come in a variety of species as well as colors; the purple to blue *Viola sororia* is the most common in the central and eastern United States. Once the petals are prepped, making the jam takes only a few minutes. The reward is a beautiful, jewel-colored freezer jam rich in vitamins A and C.

60 g / 3 packed cups violet petals, stems and green sepals removed

340 g / 1½ cups water

340 g / 1 cup mild honey

30 g / 3 tablespoons freshly squeezed lemon juice

50 g / 3 tablespoons low-/no-sugar pectin

Place a plate in the freezer for the set test (see page 21) and sterilize your jars according to the directions on page 20.

Place the violet petals and ½ cup of the water in a blender and process on high until liquefied.

Combine the honey and the remaining 1 cup of water in a small saucepan and place it over medium heat. When the mixture comes to a gentle boil, turn off the heat and stir in the petal mixture and lemon juice, then carefully sprinkle in the pectin. Bring the mixture back to a gentle boil and cook for about 1 to 2 minutes, then turn off the heat and test the jam for the set, using the chilled plate.

When the preserve reaches a setting point, ladle it into the drained, hot, sterilized jars, diligently skimming away any foam from the top and leaving about 1 inch of headspace in the jars if freezing. Position the lids and secure the rings. Let the jams come to room temperature, then store them in the refrigerator for up to 1 month or in the freezer for up to 6 months.

TRY IT WITH . . . Violet Petal Jam has a distinctively remarkable color and flavor, which is best enjoyed on a slice of **Pain de Mie** or **Buckwheat Milk Bread** with just a light slathering of butter or **Labneh**. This jam also goes very well with **Ricotta** and bright citrus flavors such as fresh or candied kumquats.

Dandelion & Turmeric Jelly

— MAKES 6 CUPS OR 3 PINTS —

This clear, golden jelly acts as a fine spring tonic. A honey-scented dandelion infusion is coupled with the earthy healing properties of turmeric, making it a wonderful aid for digestion or sore and creaky bones. Steeped as you would a tea, the mixture is then strained and heated with lemon juice, honey, sugar, and additional pectin to achieve a soft set excellent for swirling. If you omit the pectin, this recipe also makes a fantastic syrup for drizzling over Baked Pain Perdu (page 98) or using in cocktails. (Recipe shown on page 101.)

---

90 g / 2 cups dandelion blossoms, petals only

3 g / 1 teaspoon grated fresh turmeric

900 g / 4 cups water

200 g / 1 cup granulated sugar

255 g / ¾ cup mild honey

50 g / 3 tablespoons low-/no-sugar pectin

75 g / ⅓ cup freshly squeezed lemon juice

Place a plate in the freezer for the set test (see page 21) and sterilize your jars according to the directions on page 20.

Place the dandelion blossoms, turmeric, and water in a medium saucepan over medium heat. Bring to a simmer and turn off the heat. Allow to steep for at least 20 to 30 minutes or up to 2 hours, until the tea takes on a deep golden hue.

Strain the mixture through a fine-mesh sieve or jelly bag into a bowl, then return the liquid to the saucepan. You should have about 3½ cups (790 g) of liquid. Bring to a simmer over medium heat and stir in ¾ cups of the sugar, small amounts at a time, as well as the honey.

Combine the remaining ¼ cup of sugar with the pectin in a small bowl. When the sugar and honey have dissolved in the hot liquid, sprinkle the pectin mixture over the liquid and stir to combine. Bring to a boil over medium-high heat and cook for about 1 minute. Turn off the heat and check for a set, using the chilled plate.

When the preserve reaches a setting point, ladle the liquid into the drained, hot, sterilized jars and position the lids and rings. Continue with the heat processing directions on page 22.

TRY IT WITH . . . This delicate but earthy jelly is excellent served on **Buckwheat Milk Bread** with just a touch of melted butter. Try using it as a glaze for roasted or grilled fish or melting it into a curried gravy for spring vegetables. It is delicious swirled into yogurt, sprinkled with bee pollen, and served with **Skillet Toast** on the side. Pair with **Seeded Seaweed Snacking Crisps** or **Sourdough Rye Crackers** topped with **Lemony Herb Chèvre**.

Honey-Roasted
Rhubarb Compote

— MAKES 1½ CUPS OR ¾ PINT —

Rhubarb is a highly anticipated, seasonal ingredient worth waiting for all winter. Once April arrives, I obsessively check the market stands for the green-to-red, young and crisp petioles or stalks of the plant that are similar in appearance to celery, discarding the leaves before preparing. You may freeze any leftovers for when the tart and tangy vegetable is out of season, but this preparation is enough to amply serve six people.

I prefer to use Saffron and Rose–Infused Honey (page 149) to give this recipe a special touch, but orange blossom honey with a generous pinch of saffron and a dash of rose water would be a clever alternative.

---

565 g / 1¼ pounds fresh rhubarb

1 teaspoon orange zest

12 g / 1 tablespoon freshly squeezed orange juice

80 g / 4 tablespoons Saffron and Rose–Infused Honey, strained (page 149)

Pinch of fine sea salt

Preheat your oven to 375°F.

Cut the rhubarb into 2- to 3-inch pieces and place them in a large roasting pan, being careful not to overcrowd the fruit. Toss with the remaining ingredients and bake for about 10 minutes. Give a gentle stir, and continue to bake for an additional 5 to 7 minutes or until the rhubarb appears slightly caramelized but still holds its shape in a spoon.

Remove the pan from the oven and serve the compote warm or at room temperature. Keep it stored in clean jars in the refrigerator for up to 2 weeks or in the freezer for up to 6 months.

TRY IT WITH . . . The tangy, sweet flavor of this compote is excellent when spooned over **Baked Pain Perdu** or **Drop Biscuits** and topped with fresh whipped cream, **Crème Fraîche**, or **Clotted Cream**. It is a perfect companion to **Ricotta** and a whole-grain toast such as **Seeded Tahini Pain Rustique** or **Miche** for a quick, satisfying breakfast.

Strawberry & Meyer Lemon Preserves

— MAKES 4 CUPS OR 2 PINTS —

The arrival of fresh, local strawberries is always a welcome sign that true summer is just around the corner. As the flowering fruit trees begin to pop in late spring, I try and tuck away some Meyer lemons for this recipe before their season closes, as their perfumed juice and rind really set this preserve apart. You may also add ¾ to 1 teaspoon of crushed green cardamom seeds to give this beautiful ruby spread an extra exotic flair, especially if common lemons are your only choice. (Recipe shown on page 90.)

1275 g / 2¾ pounds fresh strawberries, trimmed and cut into ¼- to ½-inch pieces

600 g / 3 cups granulated sugar

3 large Meyer lemons (about 225 g)

Place the strawberries in a large preserving pot and toss them with the sugar. Juice the lemons and add the juice to the pot. Remove the remaining interior membrane of the lemons and dice the rind. Add the rind to the strawberries, stirring to combine. Cover and allow this mixture to macerate for at least 1 to 2 hours at room temperature or overnight in the refrigerator.

Place a small plate in the freezer for the set test (see page 21) and sterilize your jars according to the directions on page 20.

Bring the fruit mixture to a rolling boil over high heat, then reduce the heat to medium low. Cook for approximately 25 minutes, stirring occasionally, until the foam subsides and the mixture is reduced by about half. Turn off the heat and check for the set, using the chilled plate.

When the preserve reaches a setting point, ladle it into drained, hot, sterilized jars and position the lids and rings. Continue with the heat processing directions on page 22.

TRY IT WITH . . . This gorgeous jam is excellent served on just about any buttered and toasted bread, but I especially prefer it with the tender **Pain de Mie**, **Buckwheat Milk Bread**, or **Oat Flour Brioche**. It is a fine companion to **Pistachio Cardamom Crumb Muffins**.

Cherry, Apple & Almond Conserve

— MAKES 3 CUPS OR 1½ PINTS —

Conserves are typically made with chunks of whole fruit but set apart from jam by the inclusion of nuts. This beautiful cherry mixture includes almonds, but pistachios work just as well. If you prefer only fruit, simply omit the nuts for a sweet, garnet-colored preserve. Sweet, dark cherries are used here, but tart cherries are superb if you can source them during their short season. Consider adding an additional 100 g / ½ cup of granulated sugar if using tart cherries to encourage a proper set. (Recipe shown on page 101.)

---

1 small under-ripe green apple (about 130 g)

570 g / 2½ cups sweet cherries, stemmed and pitted

2 large lemons (about 240 g)

200 g / 1 cup granulated sugar

60 g / ½ cup almonds, toasted and coarsely chopped (optional)

10 g / 1 tablespoon amaretto-flavored liquor or Kirsch (optional)

Peel and core the apple, reserving the skins and core. Chop the apple into ½-inch pieces and place them in a medium saucepan with the cherries. Juice the lemons, reserving the lemon halves. Pour the lemon juice into the pot. Place the apple peels, core, and lemon halves on a piece of cheesecloth and tie it up into a bundle using baker's twine. Submerge the cheesecloth in the pot with the apples and cherries, cover, and let it sit at room temperature for at least 1 hour or in the refrigerator overnight. If there is not enough juice to soak the bundle, add ¼ cup of water.

Place a small plate in the freezer for the set test (see page 21) and sterilize your jars according to the directions on page 20. Bring the cherry and apple mixture to a gentle simmer over medium heat and cook for about 7 to 8 minutes or until the apples are tender. Turn off the heat and remove the cheesecloth bundle. When the bundle is cool enough to handle, carefully squeeze it over the pot, getting as much of the juice back into the pot as possible.

Stir the sugar into the fruit mixture in small amounts until all the sugar is dissolved. Place the pot over high heat and bring the conserve to a rolling boil. Skim off any foam that may accumulate on the surface and continue to cook for about 5 minutes.

Stir in the almonds, if using. Return the mixture to a boil for 3 to 4 minutes longer and test for a set, using the chilled plate.

When the conserve has thickened and passes the set test, stir in the amaretto (if using) and ladle the mixture into drained, hot, sterilized jars and position the lids and rings. Continue with the heat processing directions on page 22.

TRY IT WITH . . . This rather sweet conserve is excellent when piled onto **Baked Pain Perdu**, or served with plain **Labneh** on toast. It is a beautiful and versatile adornment for just about any loaf and is lovely served with smoked or roasted meats, such as duck or lamb. It is also delicious spooned onto a toasted and buttered **Pistachio Cardamom Crumb Muffin.**

Peach & Tea Preserves

— MAKES 4 CUPS OR 2 PINTS —

One of the most satisfying summertime experiences is sinking your teeth into the flesh of a fresh peach warmed by the sun, whose sticky juices coat your lips and sensuously tickle your chin. When I find a peach harvest of unparalleled flavor, the ripeness merits standing over a hot boiling pot to create this summertime preserve. Source peaches with flesh that slightly bruises upon a gentle squeeze. If you can find only firm fruits, leave them to ripen at room temperature for several days before making these preserves. As with tomatoes, ripe peaches should never be refrigerated, as this will dull their flavor. When in season, two wonderful substitutes for peaches are juicy apricots or pluots.

Green tea is a delicate companion to the sweetness of a peach, but I have also used Earl Grey and chamomile to great effect. Each has a distinctly different character that can be intensified or minimized with more or less steeping time. Be careful not to steep the tea for too long, and note that black tea will lend the preserves a darker hue.

To infuse the finished preserves with a subtle almond flavor that marries especially well with the green tea, place the peach pits between the layers of a dish cloth and use a hammer to crack them open. Inside lies the kernel that possesses a delicious, bitter-almond flavor. Before sealing each filled jar, press one kernel into the top inch of the preserves. Heat process according to the directions on page 22. Discard the kernel upon opening the jar, and enjoy the delicious, sweet almond flavor. Use this method for Spiced Plum Preserves (page 121) as well. (Recipe shown on page 100.)

---

565 g / 2½ cups boiling water

12 g / 4 teaspoons loose green tea leaves or
    4 green tea bags

1,020 g / 2¼ pounds ripe peaches (about 6 to 7
    large), halved and pitted (see Kitchen Note)

250 g / 1¼ cups granulated sugar

50 g / 3 tablespoons low- / no-sugar pectin

55 g / ¼ cup freshly squeezed lemon juice

Zest of 1 lemon

Place a small plate in the freezer for the set test (see page 21) and sterilize your jars according to the directions on page 20. Steep the tea for about 5 minutes in the boiling water or 8 to 10 minutes for a stronger, slightly bitter flavor.

Coarsely chop the peaches into 1-inch pieces and place them in a preserving pot. Strain the green tea through a fine-mesh sieve into the pot. Bring the tea and peaches to a boil over high heat and cook for about 3 to 4 minutes.

Remove the pot from the heat and slowly stir in 1 cup of the sugar until it is completely dissolved. Bring the preserves to a boil once again and cook for about 10 minutes.

In a small bowl, whisk the remaining ¼ cup of sugar with the pectin; set aside. Remove the pot from the heat, stir in the lemon juice, and sprinkle the pectin mixture over the preserves. Return the pot to high heat and bring the peach mixture to a rolling boil, skimming off any foam that may appear on the surface. Cook for an additional 3 to 4 minutes and test for a set, using the chilled plate.

When the preserve has passed the set test, ladle the mixture into the drained, hot, sterilized jars and position the lids and rings. Continue with the heat processing directions on page 22.

TRY IT WITH . . .   This delicate preserve is delicious served simply with butter on a variety of toasts, but it is especially nice with tender, enriched breads such as the **Pain de Mie** or **Oat Flour Brioche**. It is delightful served with savory meats, such as roasted or grilled fish on **Lavash** alongside a bed of sautéed or steamed greens such as mizuna. Try it with **Pistachio Cardamom Crumb Muffins** in the dead of winter for a little summer throwback.

KITCHEN NOTE If you are not fond of the sometimes coarse texture of peach skins, you can blanch the ripe fruits first to loosen their skins before peeling. Using a paring knife, score a shallow X on the blossom end (bottom) of the peach. Fill a large stock pot with about 12 to 14 cups of water and bring it to a boil. Carefully place the peaches in the boiling water and blanch for about 5 minutes or until the skins begin to peel back and loosen. Transfer the peaches to an ice bath to cool before peeling and discarding the skins.

Honeydew, Vanilla & Lime Jam

— MAKES 7 CUPS OR 3½ PINTS —

The scent of a ripe melon is unmistakably alluring in late summer and early fall when the pregnant fruits have swollen with sweetness on the vine. Choose melons that are heavy for their size and smell sweet when brought near to the nose; you should be able to easily spoon their flesh directly into the blender. The resulting preserve has a texture somewhere between a soft jelly and a smooth, succulent jam. I like to source Key limes whenever possible to make this jelly bright and distinctive. If you are looking for less subtlety, try pureeing the melon with 1 cup (25 g) of fresh mint leaves to lend a beautiful color and herbal character to this seasonal favorite.

1,260 g / 6 cups honeydew puree (from a
    2350-g/5-pound melon)
1 vanilla bean, split
500 g / 2½ cups granulated sugar
70 g / 4 tablespoons low-/no-sugar pectin

100 g / ½ cup freshly squeezed lime juice
2 teaspoons lime zest
40 g / 3½ tablespoons freshly squeezed
    lemon juice

Place a plate in the freezer for the set test (see page 21) and sterilize your jars according to the directions on page 20.

    Place the honeydew puree in a large saucepan. Scrape the vanilla seeds into the pan and drop in the vanilla pod. Bring the fruit to a simmer over medium heat and cook for about 5 to 6 minutes.

    Remove the pan from the heat and slowly stir in 2¼ cups of the sugar until it is completely dissolved. In a small bowl, whisk the remaining ¼ cup of sugar with the pectin; set aside.

    Return the pot to the stove over medium-high heat. Bring the mixture to a boil and cook for 8 minutes. Add the lime and lemon juice and zest. Sprinkle in the pectin mixture, stirring to combine. Return the mixture to a vigorous boil and cook for an additional 3 to 4 minutes. Turn off the heat and test for a set, using the chilled plate.

    When the jam reaches a setting point, ladle it into the hot, drained, sterilized jars. Wipe the rims, position the lids and rings, and heat process for 5 minutes according to the directions on page 22.

TRY IT WITH . . . This sweet, delicately flavored jam is an appropriate accompaniment to shaved serrano ham or other dry-cured charcuterie. If you add a handful of mint to the puree, serve alongside grilled or roasted lamb. It is also a welcome addition to any cheese plate and complements soft cheeses particularly well.

Watermelon Jelly

This firm, bubble gum–pink jelly is summer on a spoon. Break open a jar of this in mid-winter when sweaty nights and sexy beach picnics seem desperately distant. (Recipe shown on page 94.)

---

915 g / 4 cups watermelon puree, strained
(from a small, 2,000-g /4½-pound melon)
300 g / 1½ cups granulated sugar

50 g / 3 tablespoons low-/no-sugar pectin
75 g / ⅓ cup freshly squeezed lemon juice
20 g / 2 tablespoons white vinegar

Place a plate in the freezer for the set test (see page 21) and sterilize your jars according to the directions on page 20

Place the watermelon puree in a large saucepan and bring it to a simmer over medium heat, about 10 minutes. The solids will float to the top; do not skim them away at this time.

Remove the pot from the heat and slowly stir in 1¼ cups of the sugar until it is completely dissolved. In a small bowl, whisk the remaining ¼ cup of sugar and the pectin; set aside.

Return the pot to the stove over medium-high heat, bring the mixture to a boil, and cook for 10 minutes.

Remove the pot from the heat and stir in the lemon juice. Sprinkle in the pectin and sugar mixture, being careful not to add too much at once, as this may cause clumping. Stir to combine and return the mixture to a vigorous boil over high heat. Cook for an additional 3 to 4 minutes, then test for a set, using the chilled plate.

When the jelly reaches a setting point, ladle it into the hot, drained, sterilized jars. Wipe the rims, position the lids and rings, and heat process for 5 minutes according to the directions on page 22.

TRY IT WITH . . . This is an excellent spread for lightly toasted **Pain de Mie**, and it is also delicious on **A Modest Baguette** with **Labneh** or crumbled Feta and with a garnish of fresh mint. Try it served with smooth and creamy duck or chicken liver pâté.

Tomato Marmalade

— MAKES 6 CUPS OR 3 PINTS —

This fragrant marmalade is an adaptation of a recipe I first discovered in an old Time Life book of recipes from the Pacific Northwest, which was edited by James Beard back in 1970. It is best made with mostly paste tomatoes, such as San Marzano or Roma, and a few flavorful beefsteak types such as Brandywine; the cooking time will vary according to the amount of juice in the tomatoes you choose. Make this recipe at the height of summer when tomatoes are at their most flavorful and California-grown Valencia oranges are in season. (Recipe shown on page 118.)

2,950 g / 6½ pounds ripe whole tomatoes
700 g / 3½ cups granulated sugar
340 g / 1 cup mild honey
75 g / ⅓ cup freshly squeezed lemon juice
105 g / ½ cup freshly squeezed orange juice
15 g / 1½ tablespoons red wine vinegar
240 g / 2½ cups citrus peel (from about
  6 oranges, 2 grapefruit, and 2 lemons)

60 g / ½ cup peeled and finely grated
  fresh ginger
2 cinnamon sticks
1 teaspoon ground allspice
½ teaspoon fine sea salt

Bring a large pot of water to a boil. Carefully place the tomatoes in the pot and return the water to a brisk boil for about 1 to 2 minutes or until the skins begin to curl. Drain and transfer the tomatoes to an ice bath to cool. With a paring knife, peel away the skins and discard them. Coarsely chop the tomatoes, removing the cores, and place them in a large bowl. Toss the chopped tomatoes with the remaining ingredients and let the mixture rest at room temperature for at least 1 hour, or cover and refrigerate overnight.

Place a plate in the freezer for the set test and assemble your water-filled pot and jars for sterilization (see page 21). Transfer the tomato mixture to a large preserving pan and set the pan over medium-high heat. Bring the mixture to a boil, stirring constantly for about 5 minutes. Lower the heat and simmer for 1 to 1½ hours, uncovered. Stir frequently in the last half hour of cooking so the thickened marmalade won't stick to the bottom of the pan.

In the last half hour of cooking the marmalade, sterilize your jars according to the directions on page 20. When the marmalade is thick enough to hold its shape almost solidly in a spoon, test for set, using the chilled plate.

When the marmalade passes the set test, skim off and discard any foam that may appear on the surface and remove the cinnamon sticks. Ladle the marmalade into drained, hot, sterilized jars, and position the lids and rings. Heat process the jars for 10 minutes according to the directions on page 22.

TRY IT WITH . . . This distinctively fragrant and sweet marmalade is a must on any cheese board and pairs especially well in place of a chutney with roasted meats. It is also a star ingredient in **The Best Grilled Cheese Sandwich**.

Blackberry, Apple & Sage Jam

— MAKES 4½ CUPS OR 2¼ PINTS —

Blackberry picking was a favorite activity while I was growing up, as these berries grew abundantly in the hedgerows on our farm. My father cautioned me to be quiet and observant upon approaching a patch, as I might be lucky enough to spot a terrapin munching away on the berries. The promise of this decadent scene of berry-gorging turtles was all the more reason to get out early in the morning before the Southern sun's intensity made us sweat.

This recipe is best made using wild-picked berries, as their flavor at the height of summer is incomparable to store-bought, conventionally grown fruit. Use green apples that are a bit on the under-ripe side if possible, as their pectin content will help this jam to firm up once cooled. For a delicious variation, try substituting half the berries for black currants if you have access to them in season.

---

455 g / 1 pound green apples
455 g / 1 pound blackberries
One 4-inch sprig fresh sage

20 g / 2 tablespoons freshly squeezed lemon juice
700 g / 3½ cups granulated sugar

Place a plate in the freezer for the set test (see page 21) and sterilize your jars according to the directions on page 20.

Peel, core, and dice the apples into 1-inch pieces. In a large preserving pot set over medium heat, combine the diced apples with ½ cup (115 g) of water. Simmer gently for 8 to 10 minutes until the apples soften to a pulp, then use a fork to mash them in the pot.

Add the blackberries, sage, and lemon juice to the mashed apple. Continue to cook over medium heat until the blackberries release their juices, about 7 minutes.

Remove the pot from the heat and gradually stir in the sugar. When the sugar has completely dissolved, return the fruit to the stove over high heat, bring the mixture to a rapid boil, and cook for about 12 to 15 minutes. Skim off any foam that accumulates on the surface and test for a set, using the chilled plate.

When the jam passes the set test, remove and discard the sage. Ladle the jam into the hot, drained, sterilized jars and heat process for 5 minutes according to the directions on page 22.

TRY IT WITH . . . The mellow herbal notes of this jam are a delicious condiment for roasted pork sliders served on **Oat Flour Brioche** or **Pretzel Rolls**. If making pork chops, stir a few tablespoons of these preserves into the pan drippings before deglazing or making into a lush gravy, and serve with grilled or toasted **Miche** or **Drop Biscuits**. Use as an alternative to maple syrup on **Baked Pain Perdu** made with **Black Bread**.

◄ *Left to right*: Prickly Pear and Aperol Jelly; Blackberry, Apple, and Sage Jam; Tomato Marmalade; Honeydew, Vanilla, and Lime Jam; Watermelon Jelly. *Also shown*: Sourdough Rye Crackers.

Spiced Plum Preserves

— MAKES 5 CUPS OR 2½ PINTS —

This delightful jam is pleasantly spiced and balanced with a bright acidity from the lemon and vinegar. The inclusion of fresh shiso (sometimes called perilla) is a natural pairing with plums and apricots and a nod to the delicious Japanese tradition of pickling plums with shiso leaves—called *umeboshi* or *umezuke*. This weedy herb, found running wild in gardens where it's been sown or at farmers' markets in high summer, lends an herbaceous and aromatic flavor to this jam, with nuances of mint, basil, and anise.

1,360 g / 3 pounds plums, pitted and
    coarsely chopped
170 g / ½ cup mild honey
35 g / 3 tablespoons freshly squeezed
    lemon juice
10 g / 1 tablespoon plum vinegar or
    red wine vinegar

¼ teaspoon fine sea salt
3 cinnamon sticks
One 4- to 6-inch stem fresh shiso with leaves
1 vanilla bean, split
400 g / 2 cups granulated sugar

Place a plate in the freezer for the set test (see page 21) and sterilize your jars according to the directions on page 20.

In a large preserving pot, combine the plums, honey, lemon juice, vinegar, salt, cinnamon sticks, and shiso stem. Scrape the vanilla bean seeds into the pot and drop in the pod. Bring the mixture to a rolling boil over high heat, stirring occasionally, and cook for 10 minutes or until the plums soften and release their juices.

Remove the pot from the heat and gradually stir in the sugar until it is completely dissolved. Return the pot to high heat, bring the mixture back to a boil, and cook for another 20 minutes or until the preserves begin to thicken, carefully stirring in the last 10 minutes of cooking to prevent scorching. When the preserves hold their shape well in a spoon, remove the pot from the heat and test for a set, using the chilled plate. Skim off any foam that may have developed on top of the mixture and remove the cinnamon sticks, vanilla pod, and shiso stem.

When the preserve passes the set test, ladle it into the hot, drained, and sterilized jars. Wipe the rims, position the lids and rings, and heat process to seal for 5 minutes according to the directions on page 22.

TRY IT WITH . . . Serve with soft ripened cheeses, cured meats, or simply on top of buttered toast.

Sumac Jelly

Staghorn sumac (*Rhus typhina*) is a large and open-spreading deciduous shrub native to the eastern United States. It sports furry stems and erect clusters of fruit in late summer or early fall that are akin to the velvet stage of a stag's antlers. It is a picturesque plant with blazing orange autumn-leaf color, and it colonizes in groves along well-drained to dry slopes. *R. typhina* is not easily confused with poison sumac, which has distinctively different white berries and grows in swampy conditions. *R. glabra* and *R. copallinum* are two additional species of sumac found in the eastern half of the United States that are equally delicious used in this application.

This recipe uses whole clusters of sumac seeds (or drupes, as they are botanically called) to create a tart and lemony, tannic jelly high in vitamin C with a beautiful garnet color. I prefer this recipe as is, but you may wish to add a dash of cinnamon and ground allspice to accentuate its seasonal enjoyment.

Eight 4- to 6-inch-long sumac fruit clusters (315 g), rinsed
850 g / 2½ cups mild honey

½ teaspoon fine sea salt
100 g / 6 tablespoons low-/no-sugar pectin

Place the sumac and 5 cups (1,125 g) of water in a large stock pot. Bring the mixture to a gentle boil over medium-high heat, then reduce the heat to low and simmer for 20 minutes. Remove the sumac clusters and pour the liquid through a jelly bag into a large bowl; return the sumac to the pot. Add 3 cups (675 g) of water to the pot and again bring it to a gentle boil over medium-high heat. Reduce the heat to low and simmer for 10 minutes, then strain the liquid through a jelly bag into the bowl with the first batch of sumac tea. Discard the sumac or soak it in a few cups of cold water to make a mild "lemonade."

Place a plate in the freezer for the set test (see page 21) and sterilize your jars according to the directions on page 20.

Transfer 5 cups (1125 g) of the hot sumac tea into a preserving pot and stir in the honey and salt until completely dissolved. Sprinkle in the pectin, stir well, and bring the mixture to a rolling boil over high heat, skimming off any foam that accumulates on the surface. Cook for 1 to 2 minutes until the bubbles begin to visibly slow and thicken. Turn off the heat and test for a set, using the chilled plate.

When the jelly passes the set test, ladle it into the drained, hot, sterilized jars. Position the lids and rings and heat process according to the directions on page 22.

TRY IT WITH . . . This jelly is excellent served with roasted meats such as lamb or poultry. It is also perfect for **The Best Grilled Cheese Sandwich** or as a surprising addition to a cheese plate.

KITCHEN NOTE Because sumac is so high in tannic acid, this jelly will keep its set for only about 6 months. For this reason, it is best stored in the refrigerator.

Prickly Pear & Aperol Jelly

— MAKES 4 CUPS OR 2 PINTS —

Prickly pear is the fruit of the Opuntia cactus, widely distributed throughout its indigenous region in the Americas, with hardy species extending into Canada. Found also as an introduced species in the Mediterranean and Australia, it is fairly easy to source, especially in dry and arid conditions. All parts of the cactus are edible, but the varied fruits are a special treat. In Mexico, where it is often referred to as tuna, the fruit is used to make delicious agua frescas, beautiful cocktails, candies, sauces, and preserves. The pernicious spines that gave prickly pear its name can literally make them a pain to harvest in late summer or early fall, so I recommend packing a pair of salad tongs and a sharp knife with a long blade to assist—and harvest only those fruits that release easily from the cactus pads. To rid yourself of danger before making this beautiful jelly, simply position the fruit over the open flame of your stovetop to burn away the spines. If you don't have a gas stove, you can pay a pretty penny for spine-free prickly pears at your local grocery store. Markets specializing in Hispanic goods usually carry them, but I have been seeing them pop up in high-end specialty groceries as well.

The flavor of prickly pear depends on the species, and I prefer to use the crimson varieties for their impressive neon color to make this jelly. Their flavor falls somewhere between a mild watermelon and a tart kiwi. I use both a variety of citrus as well as Aperol to complement the natural flavors of the fruit. Made with bitter orange, gentian, rhubarb, and cinchona, Aperol is a subtle presence that provides a complex undertone to this jelly. (Recipe shown on page 118.)

---

840 g / about 5 large prickly pear fruits
675 to 790 g / 3 to 3½ cups water
1 teaspoon orange zest
200 g / 1 cup granulated sugar
50 g / 3 tablespoons low-/no-sugar pectin

85 g / ¼ cup mild honey
110 g / ½ cup freshly squeezed lemon juice
10 g / 1 tablespoon freshly squeezed lime juice
40 g / 4 tablespoons Aperol

Place a plate in the freezer for the set test (see page 21) and sterilize your jars according to the directions on page 20.

Quarter the fruits and place them in a large saucepan. Cover with enough water to just cover the fruit and bring to a boil over high heat. Cook until the fruit is tender, about 5 to 6 minutes. Drain, reserving the juice, and then run the soft fruit through a food mill. You should have about 4½ cups (1,215 g) of combined juice and pulp.

Transfer the juice and pulp to a large preserving pot, add the orange zest, and bring to a simmer over medium heat. Gradually add the honey and ¾ cup (150 g) of the sugar, stirring to dissolve. Combine the remaining ¼ cup of sugar with the pectin and sprinkle this mixture into the pot. Stir to dissolve, then add the lemon and lime juices and the Aperol. Return the mixture to a boil and test for a set after 1 to 2 minutes, using the chilled plate.

When the jelly passes the set test, ladle it into the drained, hot, sterilized jars and heat process for 5 minutes according to the directions on page 22. This jelly is best stored in the refrigerator to retain its set.

TRY IT WITH . . . The bright flavors of this jelly pair especially well with grilled fish or chicken in a savory expression, finished with fresh cilantro. Use as a beautiful crimson topping for any manner of toast, scones, or biscuits.

Dulce de Higos

The sensation of scent or flavor can leave us with memories forever emblazoned into our consciousness. One such experience was at an animal market I visited in Otavalo, Ecuador. Known to both tourists and locals alike for its massive Saturday gatherings, it brings the wealthiest indigenous peoples of the region to sell or trade their large and small animals. It is a spectacle of dust and hectic maneuvering, replete with panicked cries from stubborn pigs and reluctant cattle. It is an anxious scene that I had avoided for several visits to the region but which I felt, as a carnivore, I should finally witness.

The best part of the morning was spying a small vendor on my way into the market with a steaming pot of what smelled like sweet heaven compared to the more offensive aromas wafting through the field. Inside the pot were gurgling figs bobbing about in a dark, aromatic syrup. I nodded an enthusiastic yes as the vendor proudly spooned them into a soft bun with a wedge of queso fresco, shoving it toward me in exchange for a dollar coin. The spiced syrup soaked into the bread and mingled with the salty cheese to produce a taste sensation I have craved since, minus the accompanying harried sounds and smells of sheep, pigs, chickens, horses, and cattle.

These figs poached in syrup is a recipe based on that of an Ecuadorian family I have come to know, whose grandmother passed along some advice. Ecuadorians often soak their figs in water with baking soda before and after boiling them—a laborious process meant to eliminate the milky sap from the fruit before cooking them in syrup, ensuring that they are soft rather than tough and rubbery. I soak the figs once overnight in this recipe and find them to be of a pleasing texture. Sweet, dark-skinned cultivars such as "Brown Turkey," "Italian Black," or "Papa John" are best suited for this recipe, but the sweeter green-skinned selections such as "Green Ischia" will yield pleasing results.

---

500 g / about 20 large fresh figs

900 g / 4 cups water

430 g / 1 small block panela or 430 g / 2 packed cups light brown sugar

2 cinnamon sticks

½ teaspoon ground allspice

¼ teaspoon ground cloves

20 g / 2 tablespoons freshly squeezed lemon juice

Using a paring knife, score the tops of the figs with a crosswise slit. Place them in a large bowl, cover with water, and leave to bleed the sap at room temperature overnight.

The next day, sterilize the jars according to the directions on page 20.

Bring the water and panela to a boil over high heat, stirring until all the sugar is dissolved. Drain the figs and add them to the boiling water with the spices and salt. Continue boiling for 1 hour or until the syrup has reduced by about half.

Stir in the lemon juice and remove the pot from the heat. Ladle the dulce de higos into the drained, hot, sterilized jars. Position the lids and rings, and heat process according to the directions on page 22.

TRY IT WITH . . . The whole figs and syrup are excellent when served alongside a wedge of salty cheese, such as queso fresco, and wedged between a soft **Oat Flour Brioche** or **Pretzel Roll**. Spoon over **Baked Pain Perdu** or serve with **Ricotta** and a **Dry Toast** or **Skillet Toast** of your choosing.

Caramel Apple Bourbon Butter

— MAKES 4 CUPS OR 2 PINTS —

This apple butter is rich with aromatic spices, sweet with deep and nutty caramel notes, and has just enough booze to feel a little naughty. Sorghum syrup is a pantry staple of the South, but if you cannot source it, substitute with maple syrup instead.

1,135 g / 2½ pounds Granny Smith or other tart apples, quartered and cored

790 g / 3½ cups water

85 g / 6 tablespoons unsalted butter

40 g / 2 tablespoons sorghum syrup

210 g / 1 cup packed light brown sugar

20 g / 2 tablespoons freshly squeezed lemon juice

½ teaspoon fine sea salt

1 teaspoon ground cinnamon

¼ teaspoon ground mace (or nutmeg)

55 g / ¼ cup bourbon

Place the quartered apples and water in a large stock pot set over medium-high heat. Bring the mixture to a gentle boil, reduce the heat to medium low, then cover the pot and cook for about 30 minutes or until the apples are soft.

Remove the pot from the heat and strain the mixture through a fine-mesh sieve into a large bowl. Set aside the liquid and run the solids through a food mill. You should have about 2¼ cups (565 g) of apple sauce. Save the liquid to use as a pectin stock (see note on page 28 or Kitchen Note below).

Preheat the oven to 350°F. In a large, ovenproof skillet set over medium-low heat, melt the butter and stir in the sorghum syrup and sugar until completely dissolved. Cook, stirring occasionally, until the mixture begins to bubble and caramelize, about 7 to 8 minutes.

Stir in the apple sauce, lemon juice, and spices. Place the skillet in the preheated oven and bake for about 30 minutes. Take the skillet out of the oven, stir in the bourbon, and then return the skillet to the oven. Cook for another 10 to 12 minutes or until the mixture has reduced and has a deep, nutty, caramel flavor.

Ladle the apple butter into clean glass jars and position the lids. Store it in the refrigerator for up to 1 month or in the freezer for up to 1 year.

TRY IT WITH . . . If you don't eat it straight from the jar, smear it between bread slices for **The Best Grilled Cheese Sandwich** with brie, or use in roast pork sandwiches on **Pretzel Rolls**.

KITCHEN NOTE You can use the reserved apple cooking liquid to replace water in recipes such as Vanilla Marmalade or Fennel, Pear, and Black Pepper Preserves to help with the set.

Fennel, Pear & Black Pepper Preserves

— MAKES 8 CUPS OR 4 PINTS —

This sweet and peppery preserve uses the whole fennel plant to create a surprising autumnal flavor combination. I prefer to use green Kashmiri raisins for their tart flavor, but you may substitute with golden raisins, dried apricots, or even dried cranberries instead. If you wish to make this into more of a sauce, simply halve the granulated sugar.

680 g / 1½ pounds fennel bulb(s) with fronds

660 g / 3 fresh pears, cored and diced into ¼-inch pieces

150 g / 1 cup green raisins, chopped

340 g / 1½ cups water

315 g / 1½ cups freshly squeezed orange juice

75 g / ⅓ cup freshly squeezed lemon juice

9 g / 1 tablespoon orange zest

1 teaspoon coarsely ground black pepper

1,000 g / 5 cups granulated sugar

85 g / ¼ cup mild honey

Place a plate in the freezer for the set test (see page 21) and sterilize your jars according to the directions on page 20.

Peel and core the fennel bulb(s). Slice the bulb(s) lengthwise and stalks crosswise into thin strips, reserving the fronds separately. You should have about 5 cups (450 g) of sliced fennel bulb/stem and 1 packed cup (30 g) of fronds. In a large stock or preserving pot, combine the fennel bulb/stem, pears, raisins, water, citrus juices, zest, and black pepper. Bring the mixture to a gentle boil over medium-high heat and let it cook for about 15 minutes, until tender but still firm, then turn off the heat and gradually stir in the sugar and honey until they are completely dissolved.

Return the fennel mixture to a boil over medium-high heat and let it cook for 15 minutes. Turn off the heat and test for a set, using the chilled plate. If it hasn't reached its setting point, continue to cook for another 5 to 7 minutes, then test again.

When the preserve passes the set test, ladle it into the drained, hot, sterilized jars and position the lids and rings, then heat process for 10 minutes according to the directions on page 22.

TRY IT WITH . . . Grill or braise a few sausages, wedge them between a few slices of soft **Buckwheat Milk Bread** or a few **Pretzel Rolls**, and finish with this sweet preserve. Stir it into pan drippings to make a gravy or serve it alongside flaky, mild poached fish. Toast a piece of **Black Bread** or **Miche**, smear with **Ricotta**, and spoon on this preserve before garnishing with fresh fennel flowers and the reserved fruits.

Gingered Sweet Potato Butter

— MAKES ABOUT 4 CUPS OR 2 PINTS —

This beautiful, smooth, and creamy butter is the color and flavor of autumn in a jar and smells wonderful as it is being prepared. Sweet potatoes are high in B vitamins, potassium, and manganese, and a wonderful source of vitamin C and dietary fiber. So smear a little more onto your morning toast for good health!

645 g / 2⅓ cups roasted sweet potato, skins removed

115 g / 1 cup peeled, cored, and cubed (in 1-inch chunks) apples

140 g / ⅔ cup grapefruit juice

20 g / 2 tablespoons freshly squeezed lemon juice

180 g / ¾ cup sorghum syrup

2 teaspoons finely grated fresh ginger

¾ teaspoon ground cinnamon

¼ teaspoon ground nutmeg

¾ teaspoon fine sea salt

Place the roasted sweet potato, apple pieces, grapefruit juice, and lemon juice in a food processor and process on high until the mixture is relatively smooth.

Transfer the mixture to a medium saucepan, stir in the remaining ingredients, and place the pan over medium heat. Cook for about 25 to 30 minutes, stirring occasionally. The mixture will bubble, hiss, and steam like active volcanic lava. Continue cooking until the mixture thickens and smells fragrantly caramelized, stirring often toward the end to prevent scorching.

Transfer the sweet potato butter to clean jars and store them in the refrigerator for up to 1 month.

TRY IT WITH . . . This comforting spread is delicious when served on toast with simply a pat of butter. It pairs especially well with **Spiced Carrot Levain** and **Black Bread** but is versatile enough to accompany most loaves. Make it a little savory by sprinkling some Feta or blue cheese over top and garnishing with fresh microgreens.

◀ *In jars, left to right*: Cranberry, Apricot, and Apple Mostarda; Gingered Sweet Potato Butter. *On spoons, left to right*: Spiced Concord Grape Jam; Gingered Sweet Potato Butter; Fennel, Pear, and Black Pepper Preserves; Dulce de Higos; Cranberry, Apricot, and Apple Mostarda. *Also shown*: Oat Flour Brioche.

Spiced Concord Grape Jam

— MAKES 4 CUPS OR 2 PINTS —

I wait anxiously for Concord grapes all summer, until they finally arrive at the greenmarket. Cold-hardy, vigorous, and fairly resistant to blight, they encompass one of my favorite child-hood memories, rambling their way onto the side of my grandmother's front porch where we could watch them swell and ripen in the crisp October air. Their foxy, full-bodied flavor is unparalleled in intensity and is fortunately high in pectin, making it the perfect varietal for making jam. (Recipe shown on page 132.)

1,360 g / 3 pounds Concord grapes
600 g / 3 cups granulated sugar
55 g / ¼ cup freshly squeezed lemon juice

FOR THE BOUQUET GARNI
2 tablespoons fresh rosemary, coarsely chopped
6 whole dried juniper berries
2 bay leaves
2 whole cloves

Place a plate in the freezer for the set test (see page 21) and sterilize and prepare your jars according to the directions on page 20.

Separate the grape skins from the interior pulp by popping them in between your thumb and forefinger. Place the skins into a food processor or blender along with ½ cup (100 g) of the sugar and process until a thin slurry forms.

To make the bouquet garni, place the rosemary, juniper berries, bay leaves, and cloves on a piece of cheesecloth and tie it up in a bundle using baker's twine. Place the pulp from the grapes in a medium saucepan and drop in the bouquet garni. Bring the mixture to a light simmer over medium heat. Remove the pan from the heat and gradually stir in the remaining sugar until it is completely dissolved. Return the pan to the stovetop over medium-high heat and bring it to a gentle boil. Cook for about 20 minutes, until it slightly thickens, skimming off any foam that may form on the surface. Remove the pan from the heat and discard the bouquet garni.

Run the boiled grape mixture through a food mill, then return it to the pan along with the processed skins. Stir in the lemon juice and place the pan over medium heat. Cook for another 20 minutes or so, then test the jam for a set, using the chilled plate.

When the jam passes the set test, ladle it into the drained, hot, sterilized jars. Position the lids and rings and heat process for 5 minutes according to the directions on page 22.

TRY IT WITH . . . Spiced with a bouquet of aromatic flavors, this jam makes a fancy PB&J between slices of **Pain de Mie** or is delicious on a modest serving of **Olive Oil Cake**. Pair it with **Cinnamon-Hazelnut Butter** on **Skillet-Toasted Miche** for a hearty snack or breakfast.

Cranberry, Apricot & Apple Mostarda

— MAKES 4 CUPS OR 2 PINTS —

This zippy fruit condiment, which hails from Northern Italy, is a beautiful addition to any charcuterie or cheese plate. Earthy spices mingle with the sweet fruit, and a jolt of bold mustard pungency brings a complexity to this versatile preserve. Prepare in autumn when cranberries are abundant and reasonably priced, although frozen cranberries will work just as well. (Recipe shown on page 132.)

160 g / ¾ cup apple cider vinegar

60 g / ¼ cup water

55 g / ¼ cup freshly squeezed orange juice

255 g / ¾ cup mild honey or Infused Honey (page 149)

50 g / ¼ cup granulated sugar

1 cinnamon stick

2 bay leaves

¼ teaspoon ground cloves

½ teaspoon ground allspice

340 g / 4 cups fresh or frozen cranberries, thawed

170 g / 1½ cups finely chopped apple of your choice

100 g / ¾ cup dried apricots, diced

60 g / 4 tablespoons prepared grainy mustard

½ teaspoon orange zest

1 teaspoon fresh thyme leaves

Sterilize your jars according to the directions on page 20.

Place the vinegar, water, orange juice, honey, and sugar in a large saucepan over medium heat. Stir in the spices and heat until the sugar is completely dissolved. Add the remaining ingredients and simmer for about 35 minutes or until the mixture becomes thick, stirring frequently in the last 10 minutes to prevent scorching. Discard the cinnamon stick and bay leaves.

Ladle the mixture into the hot, drained, sterilized jars and heat process for 5 minutes according to the directions on page 22. Store in a cool location for up to 1 year.

TRY IT WITH . . . Pair with creamy cheeses served at room temperature or your favorite cured meats for a delicious holiday entertaining spread. This mostarda is also delicious used on **The Best Grilled Cheese Sandwich** prepared with a mild Cheddar. Mostarda of any sort is excellent served throughout the winter holidays, when our attention turns to roasted meats and hearty flavors.

Onion, Thyme & Date Jam

— MAKES ABOUT 1¾ CUP OR ¾ PINT —

A little of this complex, caramelized jam goes a long way, but it's so surprisingly addictive, you'll be reaching for another spoon before you realize it is made with onions! I have used other fruits in this recipe—including dried figs and raisins—with delicious results, but dates work really well to thicken the jam. For another version, try soaking the dried fruit overnight in 3 tablespoons of brandy or bourbon before using in this recipe. Although it's not necessary for a delicious result, it adds a robust, boozy layer of flavor perfectly suited to rustic, country-style meat pâtés. (Recipe shown on page 138.)

360 g / 3 cups thinly sliced red or sweet onion
 (such as Vidalia)

¾ teaspoon fine sea salt

30 g / 2 tablespoons vegetable oil

½ teaspoon coarsely ground black pepper

1 large sprig thyme

115 g / ½ cup water

60 g / 3 tablespoons mild honey

30 g / 3 tablespoons apple cider vinegar

½ teaspoon orange zest

120 g / ¾ cup pitted dates, chopped

20 g / 2 tablespoons brandy or bourbon
 (optional)

In a heavy-bottomed skillet set over medium heat, sauté the onions and salt in the oil until they are soft and translucent, about 8 minutes.

Add the black pepper, thyme, water, honey, vinegar, zest, and dates, reduce the heat to low, and cook until the dates thicken and the onions soften considerably, about 18 to 20 minutes, stirring frequently near the end to prevent scorching.

Stir in the brandy and continue cooking for about 5 to 7 more minutes. The jam will be ready when the dates have thickened into almost a paste and the onions are caramelized.

Remove the thyme sprig and store the jam in a lidded container in the refrigerator for up to 1 month. Serve warm or at room temperature.

TRY IT WITH . . . This jam falls lusciously between sweet and savory and is wonderful served in a variety of ways to accompany pâtés, cured meats, or cheese plates alongside **Fermented Grainy Mustard**. Use it to adorn **The Best Grilled Cheese Sandwich** made with **Black Bread**, **Spiced Carrot Levain**, or **Miche**. It is a surprisingly appropriate candidate for pairing with **Soft Pretzels**. Spread it on **Garlic Crostini** and finish with a variety of fresh garnishes, such as cilantro and shaved radishes.

Vanilla Marmalade

— MAKES 8 CUPS OR 4 PINTS —

In 2014, I decided to leave my full-time horticultural job in pursuit of a seasonal lifestyle that would allow for winter travel. My preferred locations usually involve warm beaches, temperate mountain ranges, and copious amounts of ripe fruit littering roadsides and spilling forth from market stalls. I find the abundance of fresh and exotic foods incredibly inspiring and often return home with recipe ideas to keep me busy in the last weeks of winter.

One winter I worked at an upscale Hacienda near Otavalo, Ecuador, where I was spoiled by a beautiful kitchen garden replete with a small citrus grove. I marveled at the lichen-covered branches and was intoxicated by the heady blossoms overhead. I cultivated a great fondness for picking fruits directly from the tree and tearing them open to test for ripeness. After returning stateside, I longed for the companionship of those trees and their fresh, fragrant oils that stained my fingers and burned my hasty lips.

In the last month of winter, when we are desperate for a spot of sunshine, making marmalade fills the kitchen with a little tropical playfulness. Although Seville oranges have the most favorable flavor for making marmalade, they aren't always easy to source organically. Use whatever spray-free citrus you can find, with taut, blemish-free skins that feel heavy in the hand. My favorite is a combination of grapefruit, blood oranges, navel oranges, Cara Cara oranges, and Meyer lemons, whose sweetness is then balanced with a secret ingredient: cocktail bitters. I prefer grapefruit bitters, but you can experiment with other flavors, adding ½ teaspoon at a time until you achieve the right balance.

1,590 g / 3½ pounds mixed citrus fruits
100 g / 2 medium lemons
850 g / 3½ cups citrus juice
   (from the above fruit)
450 g / 2 cups water

1,900 g / 9½ cups granulated sugar
1 plump vanilla bean
¾ teaspoon grapefruit bitters

Halve the citrus and lemons and juice them, reserving 3½ cups (850 g) of the juice. Remove any remaining pulp from the citrus halves, reserving any seeds. Wrap the juiced lemon halves and any seeds in a cheesecloth (the pith and seeds contain pectin that will help the marma-lade set). Shred, slice, or chop the remaining citrus peel to your preference and transfer it to a large preserving pot. Cover the shredded or chopped peels with the reserved juice and water. Using baker's twine, tie the cheesecloth in a bundle around the juiced lemon halves and seeds, then place it in the pot. Cover and allow to sit overnight at room temperature.

The next day, place a plate in the freezer for the set test (see page 21) and sterilize your jars according to the directions on page 20. Preheat the oven to 250°F.

Measure the sugar into a heatproof bowl and place it in the oven to warm.

Bring the pot of citrus to a relaxed boil over medium-high heat, then reduce the heat to low and simmer for 30 to 45 minutes or until the mixture has reduced by about one-third and the peel is completely tender. Turn off the heat and remove the cheesecloth bag from the pot. Using the back of a large spoon, press the cheesecloth into a fine-mesh sieve positioned over a bowl, releasing as much pectin-rich liquid as possible. Transfer this liquid back to the pot. Split the vanilla bean, scrape the seeds into the pot, and toss in the pod. Gradually stir in the warmed sugar until it is completely dissolved. Add the cocktail bitters and return the pot to medium-high heat. Bring the mixture to a relaxed boil and let it cook for 20 to 40 minutes, gently stirring only occasionally to prevent scorching. Test for a set after 15 to 20 minutes, using the chilled plate. If it hasn't set after 20 minutes, continue cooking the marmalade until it is ready (this may take another 15 to 20 minutes, depending on the pectin content of the fruit).

Once it passes the set test, turn off the heat. Allow the marmalade to rest for a few minutes, then stir well and ladle it into the drained, hot, sterilized jars, being careful to include balanced amounts of peel and syrup in each jar. Position the lids and rings and heat process for 5 minutes according to the directions on page 22.

TRY IT WITH . . . This beautiful marmalade makes a delicious accompaniment to both sweet and savory dishes and is perfect for **Currant Cream Scones**. I particularly appreciate it on **Spiced Carrot Levain**, as its bright citrus flavors and gentle vanilla presence balance the spice of the bread. It is also excellent on **Black Bread** or **Sourdough Rye Crackers** with a little **Ricotta**, or adorned with butter on thinly sliced **Buttermilk Rye**.

◄ *On spoons, left to right*: Kaya Jam; Tamarind Rum Jam; Gingered Guava and Chili Preserves; Vanilla Marmalade; Onion, Thyme, and Date Jam. *In jar*: Vanilla Marmalade. *Also shown*: Spelt English Muffins.

Gingered Guava & Chili Preserves

— MAKES 2 CUPS (540 G) OR 1 PINT —

Fascinated by all things fermentation, one winter I arranged to visit a coffee-growing country to observe and participate in the field-to-cup process. When I arrived in the Quindío region of Colombia, I was awestruck by the beauty and fertility of the countryside. The hills were layered with so many shades of green, I often took my morning coffee dreamily staring out at the Andean canopy, trying to identify the many populations of vegetation that dotted the countryside.

The family farm I visited roasted small-batch coffees from shade-grown beans that had taken asylum on their property more than fifty years ago—a long time in the history of mostly large-scale Colombian production. They were located down a long, bumpy, and grinding road that I traversed in a Willys jeep. After arriving tousled and dusty, I sat on their open veranda, sipping coffee and watching the birds flit about while discussing the importance of slow living; it was an experience I will always reflect upon with great fondness and gratitude.

During my stay, my limited Spanish would ignite in quick staccato punctuation whenever our discussion turned to the flavor and the botanical distinction of coffee varieties. This small family taught me how to pick, clean, ferment, and slowly roast my own beans over an open flame, noting the subtle changes in aroma as they transformed into the dark beans with which we are familiar.

I chose to return home by walking down the remote road across field and stream to ponder the experience. Along the way, I noticed plants and fruits I had not had the opportunity to forage as of yet. Heavy, drooping trees laden with guava studded the roadside. The aromatic fruits yielded easily to my grasp, and when torn open, they revealed a beautiful pink flesh whose scent was a heady mixture of rose and pine resin. I gobbled all that I could, spitting out the hard little seeds and collecting those that indicated their ripeness by falling from the branch with a gentle nudge. In my small guesthouse kitchen, I cooked them down with a bit of sugar. They seemed to be the essence of those green studded hills, much in the same way that the coffee reflected the terroir of the soil.

When I arrived back in New York, I found an abundance of guava at the Latino markets and even in Chinatown. They were a different Mexican variety, yellow skinned and white fleshed when ripe but distinctively similar in fragrance and flavor. I processed them in much the same way as I had in Colombia, but with the addition of candied ginger and chilies for a spicy kick. (Recipe shown on page 138.)

700 g / 1½ pounds small Mexican guavas
(about 16) (see Kitchen Note)
60 g / ¼ cup water
150 g / 1¼ cups candied ginger, coarsely chopped

60 g / 3 tablespoons mild honey
25 g / 2 tablespoons freshly squeezed
lemon juice
1 fresh hot chili (or to taste)

Sterilize your jars according to the directions on page 20.

Remove the blossom ends of the guavas and quarter the fruit. Place them into a medium saucepan and add the water. Cook over medium-low heat, stirring frequently to avoid scorching, until the guavas begin to break down and become thick, about 8 to 9 minutes.

Transfer the guavas to a food mill and crank them through a fine sieve until you have about 2 cups (480 g) of pulp. Clean the saucepan and return the guava pulp. Stir in the remaining ingredients and cook over low heat, stirring frequently. The mixture will bubble and hiss much like volcanic lava. When it has thickened considerably into a chunky paste (after about 25 to 30 minutes), ladle it into drained, hot, sterilized jars, position the lids and rings, and heat process for 10 minutes according to the directions on page 22.

TRY IT WITH . . . This strongly spiced preserve works incredibly well as a marinade ingredient or a condiment for roasted meats, especially pork, duck, and chicken. It is also delicious on **The Best Grilled Cheese Sandwich** with somewhat salty cheese, such as mozzarella or queso fresco.

> **KITCHEN NOTE** To judge the ripeness of Mexican guavas, gently squeeze them. They should yield slightly and will bruise easily if handled aggressively. A fingernail should easily pierce their thin skins, and they will smell heady and ripe when ready to make into preserves.

Kaya Jam (Coconut Jam)

— MAKES 1¾ CUP (455 G) OR ABOUT 1 PINT —

This rich, only moderately sweet "jam" is a delicacy of Southeast Asian cuisine and falls somewhere between the caramel flavor of dulce de leche and the texture of a silky coconut curd or crème anglaise. It is one of my favorite sweetened recipes in this book, but requires constant attention during the cooking process. The results are so satisfying, however, that you will be delighted with the time spent to prepare this nutty spread full of toasted coconut flavor. Using freshly made coconut milk is of course preferable, but canned, full-fat coconut milk is a suitable alternative.

Pandan leaves are traditionally used to flavor this jam, although they are an obscure ingredient to find fresh. If you are lucky enough to have a market nearby that carries them, try adding three large leaves to the mixture while cooking, then discard them before storing the jam in jars. If pandan is unavailable to you, this recipe is incredibly delicious prepared without it.

400 g / one 14-ounce can full-fat coconut milk
155 g / 1 cup granulated coconut sugar

80 g / 5 large egg yolks
Pinch of fine sea salt

Combine the coconut milk and sugar in a bain-marie set over medium-low heat. Cook until the sugar dissolves and the mixture feels hot when dabbed onto your inner wrist, about 5 to 6 minutes. Meanwhile, lightly whisk the egg yolks in a medium bowl. While whisking constantly, slowly pour about 1 cup of the hot milk mixture into the egg yolks, then slowly whisk the warm egg yolk mixture back into the remaining hot milk. Continue cooking over low heat for about 45 minutes, whisking continuously to prevent the mixture from curdling. When the coconut jam has thickened to a pudding-like consistency and reduced by about one-third, strain it through a fine-mesh sieve into clean jars. Seal the jars and place them in the refrigerator for 3 to 4 hours to set. The jam will keep for up to 1 week in the refrigerator.

TRY IT WITH . . . The rich, nutty coconut flavor of this jam goes incredibly well with **Oat Flour Brioche** or **Baked Pain Perdu** prepared with the bread of your choosing. Traditionally, it is slathered on sandwiches made with a soft white bread, such as **Pain de Mie** or **Buckwheat Milk Bread**, served with soft-boiled eggs and soy sauce on the side. I prefer it on toast with grapefruit or Cara Cara orange segments garnished with fresh mint or toasted coconut.

Tamarind Rum Jam

— MAKES 4 CUPS OR 2 PINTS —

Tamarind is a fruit I learned to love in the Caribbean for its characteristically bold, sour flavor. Although native to tropical Africa, *Tamarus indica* is one of the most widely distributed trees of the tropics. It is deeply appreciated in the landscape for its beautifully graceful, drooping canopy full of finely pinnate leaflets that quiver in the breeze and fold into themselves at night. The fruit is a large and flat, bean-like pod with cinnamon-colored skin when ripe and sticky, date-like flesh. When sourcing tamarind pods, be aware that there are two different types available in commerce: sweet and sour. The one used here is the sour version, which requires a good amount of sugar to make into a pleasing jam. You may also find tamarind already processed in block forms with or without the seeds. To use the block form in this recipe, simply break it into small chunks before soaking. If you don't have coconut sugar on hand, substitute with packed light brown sugar instead. Finally, avoid making a hot mess in your kitchen by using a wide and fairly deep preserving pot with a lid for this recipe, as the thick mixture will erupt, bubble, and hiss as it cooks down. (Recipe shown on page 138.)

---

900 g / sour tamarind block (or about 60 pods)
1,810 g / about 8 cups boiling water
105 g / ½ cup freshly squeezed orange juice
85 g / ¼ cup mild honey
1 teaspoon finely grated fresh ginger

1 teaspoon ground cinnamon
½ teaspoon ground allspice
¾ teaspoon fine sea salt
300 g / 2 cups granulated coconut sugar
50 g / 5 tablespoons spiced rum

Place the whole tamarind pods or small processed tamarind chunks in a large, heatproof bowl and pour over the boiling water to cover. Allow to steep for about 30 to 45 minutes, or until the pulp of the tamarind is soft and cool. Pour off the soaking water, reserving about 1½ cups (345 g). Slip as many of the large seeds out of the pulp as you can before running the fruit through a food mill. This process should result in about 2 cups (480 g) of pulp. (Alternatively, purchase pre-processed pulp without the seeds and measure accordingly.)

Sterilize your jars according to the directions on page 20.

Place the tamarind pulp in a deep pot and add the reserved tamarind water, orange juice, honey, spices, and salt, stirring to combine. Place the pot over medium-low heat and stir in the sugar, ½ cup at a time, until it is completely dissolved.

Cover the pot and continue cooking the jam for about 1 hour over low heat, stirring occasionally to avoid scorching. When the jam thickens and holds its shape on a spoon, remove it from the heat and stir in the rum.

Ladle the jam into the drained, hot, sterilized jars, position the lids and rings, and heat process for 5 minutes according to the directions on page 22.

TRY IT WITH . . . This dark, flavorful jam is a treat served on its own with a little butter, and it's also delicious paired with roasted meats, such as pork or grilled fish and chicken. Stir it into yogurt and top with toasted coconut.

Make a quick and easy marinade or BBQ sauce by stirring together 2 parts Tamarind Rum Jam to one part apple cider vinegar, one part pureed mango, and one part chopped onion. Add a few dollops of both **Harissa** and **Fermented Grainy Mustard** to taste. To round out the flavor, stir in a few dashes of tamari to balance the sweet, spicy, and sour flavors. Serve on **Oat Flour Brioche** buns or **Pain de Mie** with roast pork or chicken and top with a crispy slaw made with **Homemade Mayonnaise**.

> **KITCHEN NOTE** Any remaining water left over from steeping the tamarind is excellent to make into a light lemonade-flavored drink sweetened with a little honey. It is also an excellent ingredient to ferment with water kefir or a kombucha mother.

4

Sweet Spreads & Nut Butters

Tʜɪs ᴄʜᴀᴘᴛᴇʀ ᴄᴏɴᴛɪɴᴜᴇs the exploration into flavor by maximizing the use of alternative sweeteners and robust, freshly ground seeds and nuts. Use these recipes as ingredients to enhance others in this book, or on their own as simple adornments to baked goods.

◄ *Top, left to right:* Pain de Mie, Spelt English Muffins, Infused Honey, Spelt English Muffins. *Bottom, left to right:* Matcha Nut Butter, Roasted Banana and Chocolate Nut Butter, Cinnamon-Hazelnut Butter, Tahini Sauce.

Infused Honey

— MAKES ABOUT 1 CUP OR ½ PINT —

Honey infused with herbs and spices is an incredibly easy way to add flavor to your cupboard. The combinations are limited only by the season and your imagination, but the following are a few of my favorites. Set them on a sunny windowsill while infusing for a beautiful presentation in the kitchen, reminding you to reach for them when you're craving something a tad bit sweet!

FOR SAFFRON, ROSE, AND PINK PEPPERCORN

15 g / ¼ cup dried rose buds

1 large pinch of saffron threads

1 teaspoon whole pink peppercorns

340 g / 1 cup mild honey

FOR SMOKY CARDAMOM, JUNIPER, AND ANISE SEED

3 whole black cardamom pods, split

½ tablespoon whole juniper berries, crushed with a mortar and pestle

½ teaspoon whole anise seeds

340 g / 1 cup mild honey

FOR VANILLA ORANGE SPICE

1 cinnamon stick

1 vanilla bean, split

1 tablespoon finely julienned orange peel

3 dried piquin or "bird's eye" chilies, split

1 teaspoon whole allspice berries, crushed with a mortar and pestle

2 whole star anise pods

340 g / 1 cup mild honey

Sterilize your jar according to the directions on page 20.

Place your herbs and spices in the sterilized jar, then pour in the honey and gently stir until all the ingredients are incorporated. Screw on the lid and place the jar in a warm location to infuse for at least 1 week, or longer for a stronger flavor. If the herbs and spices float to the top, simply stir them back in with a clean spoon. When the honey has infused to your flavor preference, strain it into another sterilized jar. Cover and store indefinitely.

TRY IT WITH . . . The uses for infused honey are endless, from stirring into hot tea to using in baked goods or jams. My favorite is to drizzle a little onto warm, freshly made **Ricotta** on a piece of **Dry Toast**. Use the saffron, rose, and pink peppercorn variation as an ingredient in **Honey-Roasted Rhubarb Compote** to serve with **Drop Biscuits** and whipped cream. The smokey cardamom, juniper, and anise seed variation is excellent when used as an ingredient in the **Cranberry, Apricot, and Apple Mostarda**.

> **KITCHEN NOTE** If foraging or collecting herbs from your garden, be sure to fully dry the herbs before use to inhibit the chance of bacterial growth in the honey. Chopping the fresh herbs before drying them will speed up the infusion process but will be more difficult to strain.

Coconut Syrup

— MAKES ABOUT ¾ CUP (220 G) —

This vegan simple syrup has a neutral sweetness similar to the flavor of panela or brown sugar. It can be used when a milder, toasted flavor is preferred, or to substitute for maple syrup, honey, or molasses. Coconut sugar is high in vitamins, minerals, and amino acids, as it is harvested from the coconut flower itself. Just be sure to source a product that is sustainably grown and gentle on our tropical environments.

---

115 g / ½ cup water   155 g / 1 cup coconut sugar

Bring the water to a boil in a medium saucepan. Stir in the coconut sugar and continue boiling until frothy, about 2 to 3 minutes. Turn off the heat and transfer the mixture into a clean jar. Store at room temperature for up to 6 months.

TRY IT WITH . . . Use this simple syrup as an ingredient in **Roasted Banana and Chocolate Nut Butter** or to replace honey in most recipes, including **Cinnamon-Hazelnut Butter**, **Fermented Grainy Mustard**, and **Harissa**. You may also use it in place of molasses in **Black Bread**, but it will produce a milder, less pronounced flavor.

Roasted Banana & Chocolate Nut Butter

— MAKES 1 CUP OR ½ PINT —

This dairy-free nut butter is a delightful treat smeared onto toast or unapologetically licked from a spoon. Studded with flakes of sea salt and a subtle banana flavor, this decadent ganache-like spread is low in refined sugar and full of healthy fats. It is not necessary to soak the nuts overnight, but it does help with digestibility if you are sensitive. If using unsoaked nuts, you will need to process a bit longer for the nutmeat to release its oils and turn into butter.

70 g / ½ cup raw almonds or cashews

125 g / 1 large overripe banana, sliced into
   1-inch pieces

35 g / 2 tablespoons packed brown sugar

85 g / 3 ounces bittersweet chocolate, grated or
   finely chopped

50 g / ¼ cup coconut oil

115 g / ⅓ cup maple syrup or Coconut Syrup
   (page 151)

½ teaspoon vanilla extract

¼ teaspoon flaked sea salt

Place the almonds or cashews in a small bowl and cover them with water. Leave to soak at room temperature overnight.

The next day, preheat your oven to 425°F. Combine the bananas and brown sugar in a parchment-lined baking dish and roast for about 20 minutes, stirring halfway through, until the bananas show caramelization. Remove the baking dish from the oven and stir in the grated chocolate until it is melted and smooth.

Drain the nuts and place them in a food processor with the coconut oil; process on high until a buttery, somewhat smooth paste forms, about 5 minutes. Add the chocolate-banana mixture, sweetener, and vanilla to the food processor and continue processing until the butter is smooth. Remove the blade and gently stir in the flaked sea salt. Transfer the nut butter into lidded jars and serve at room temperature for an easily spreadable butter, or refrigerate for a thicker, ganache-like consistency. The nut butter will keep for up to 1 month in the refrigerator.

TRY IT WITH . . . Bring to room temperature before spreading onto **Miche, Seeded Tahini Pain Rustique, A Modest Baguette,** or **Pain de Mie,** and layer fresh banana, tart red currants, or tart cherries on top. Drizzle with maple syrup or honey and finish with chopped nuts or toasted coconut.

Cinnamon-Hazelnut Butter

— MAKES 1 CUP (330 G) OR ½ PINT —

This barely sweet and easy-to-prepare nut butter has a much gentler price tag than what you might purchase readymade. Customize it to your own taste, adding more or less honey and cinnamon as you like.

280 g / 2 cups hazelnuts, toasted, skins removed
40 g / 2 tablespoons mild honey or Coconut Syrup (page 151)
10 g / 2 teaspoons neutral oil (such as grapeseed or sunflower)

½ teaspoon ground cinnamon
½ teaspoon fine sea salt

Place all the ingredients in the bowl of a food processor and blend on high until a smooth butter forms, about 8 to 10 minutes, scraping down the sides every few minutes. The mixture will progress from a crumble to a paste, and finally into a wonderfully smooth butter. Transfer the nut butter to a clean container and store it in the refrigerator for up to 2 months.

TRY IT WITH . . . This nut butter pairs especially well with the deep, toasted flavors of the whole grains used in **Miche**, **Buttermilk Rye**, **Black Bread**, and **Seeded Tahini Pain Rustique**, but it is also appropriate with **A Modest Baguette**. Top with fresh fruit such as ripened pear, figs, or crisp apple and drizzle with a little honey. My favorite mid-afternoon treat is a slice of **Chocolate and Orange Sourdough** with a smattering of this spread.

Matcha Nut Butter

— MAKES 1 CUP OR ½ PINT —

This beautiful dairy-free spread is rich and delicate with flavors of macadamia, cashew, coconut, and green tea. Packed with healthy fats and antioxidants, its light-green color makes for a wonderful and surprising presentation at the table. It is not necessary to soak the nuts overnight, but it does help with digestibility if you are sensitive. If using unsoaked nuts, you will need to process a bit longer for the nutmeat to release its oils and turn into butter. (Recipe shown on page 146.)

75 g / ½ cup macadamia nuts
70 g / ½ cup cashew nuts
50 g / ¼ cup coconut oil
115 g / ⅓ cup mild honey

7 g / ¾ tablespoon freshly squeezed lemon juice
2 teaspoons matcha powder
Pinch of fine sea salt

Place the macadamia nuts and cashews in a small bowl and cover with water. Leave to soak at room temperature overnight.

Drain the nuts and place them in the bowl of a food processor, along with the coconut oil. Process on high until a thick, creamy paste forms, about 5 to 6 minutes. Add the remaining ingredients and continue processing until you have a smooth butter. Transfer the nut butter to clean, lidded jars and chill in the refrigerator to thicken before serving. It will keep in the refrigerator for up to 2 months.

TRY IT WITH . . . This addictive spread is delicious served on all manner of toast, but I particularly love it with **Seeded Tahini Pain Rustique**, **Miche**, **Pain de Mie**, or **Spelt English Muffins**. Pair it with fresh fruit and finish with hemp seeds, toasted coconut, or cacao nibs. You may also take it to the savory side with fresh sliced radishes, pea shoots, edible flowers, and a sprinkling of **Citrus Salt**, which makes for a stunning presentation.

Tahini Sauce

When I moved to Kentucky and then to the Rockaways, there were more than a few times when I simply could not source good-quality tahini that didn't have a rancid or bitter after-taste. I began making my own when I realized how simple it was to make an ingredient I use so often taste so much better. You can include whatever oil suits your preference: an extra-virgin for a more pronounced, fruity, olive flavor or a lighter vegetable oil if you prefer the sesame to have a more forward presence. If you would rather make this sauce into a paste, cut down the oil to 2 tablespoons, but I find this is a great, all-around recipe for most applications. (Recipe shown on page 147.)

---

130 g / 1 cup raw, hulled sesame seeds

About ½ teaspoon fine sea salt, to taste

55 to 70 g / ¼ to ⅓ cup extra-virgin olive oil

FOR THE SWEET VARIATION

2:1 ratio of Tahini Sauce to honey, maple syrup, or Coconut Syrup (page 151)

FOR THE SAVORY VARIATION

110 g / ½ cup Tahini Sauce

8 g / 1 plump garlic clove, minced

10 g / 1 tablespoon freshly squeezed lemon juice

1 tablespoon chopped fresh tender herbs, such as parsley, chives, or cilantro

Place the seeds in a heavy skillet over medium-low heat and toast for about 5 minutes until fragrant and light brown, stirring occasionally. Remove the skillet from the heat and allow the seeds to cool, then transfer them to the bowl of a food processor, along with the salt. Process on high until a dry paste forms, about 3 minutes. With the blade running, slowly drizzle in the oil and continue processing until a smooth sauce forms. Store the tahini in a sealed container in the refrigerator for up to 3 months. If the oil separates, simply stir it back into the sauce before using.

For the Savory or Sweet Variations, simply mix the appropriate proportions in a small bowl and serve.

TRY IT WITH . . . Use as an ingredient in hummus for an unparalleled creamy, nutty, sesame flavor. Dress up sautéed greens with tahini and a squeeze of lemon before mounding them onto an open-faced sandwich with a dusting of **Dukkah**. Make your toast fancy with the Sweet Variation before arranging fresh fruit on top. Use the Savory Variation to garnish **Grilled Escarole** or **Sorghum-Roasted Carrots**. Don't forget to try it as an ingredient in the **Seeded Tahini Pain Rustique**!

5

Savory Spreads & Condiments

Eating delicious and satisfying food for every meal can be easy when you prepare fresh ingredients in advance. Many of the recipes in this chapter can be made in batches ahead of time, for those moments when you need to reach for a quick lunch or an impromptu snack board. Others, such as flavored salts, are wonderful additions to any pantry, effectively adding flavor to your creations with only a slight twist of the hand or wave of the spoon. Make the simplest condiments from scratch and be surprised by the glorious improvement of flavor that can be savored with such minimal effort.

◄ *Top, left to right*: Preserved Lemon and Fava Bean Hummus; Baccalà Mantecato; Blushing Goat Spread; Spicy Cheddar, Almond, and Olive Ball. *Middle*: S'chug. *Bottom, left to right*: Buckwheat Milk Bread, Rainbow Relish, Crema de Carciofi.

Lemony Herb Chèvre

— MAKES ABOUT ½ CUP —

This staple spread is so easy to prepare, I almost hesitate to offer a recipe! You may substitute the fresh tender herbs for others you have on hand, such as chervil, cilantro, or basil, depending on the season. The chives do add a pleasantly piquant layer of flavor, though, so I do suggest you seek them out.

---

115 g / ½ cup goat cheese, softened

30 g / 2 tablespoons extra-virgin olive oil or
   softened unsalted butter

½ teaspoon lemon zest

5 g / 1 teaspoon fine sea salt

3 tablespoons chopped fresh parsley

3 tablespoons chopped fresh chives

40 g / ¼ cup pistachios, toasted
   and chopped

Place the goat cheese and olive oil in a small bowl and whip with a spoon until creamy. Add the lemon zest, salt, and herbs, stirring well to combine. Transfer the mixture to a piece of parchment paper and shape it into a ball or log. Wrap it tightly in plastic and chill in the refrigerator for at least 1 hour. Place the nuts on a dish or in a shallow bowl. When the chèvre has stiffened, roll it in the nuts to coat. Alternatively, you may simply place the chèvre in a decorative jar to serve, with the nuts sprinkled on top. It will keep for up to 1 week refrigerated in a sealed container.

TRY IT WITH . . . Serve on a bed of **S'chug** or paired with **Onion, Thyme, and Date Jam**. Excellent with crusty, hearth-style breads such as the **Miche, A Modest Baguette**, or **Spiced Carrot Levain**, or smeared onto **Garlic Crostini** and topped with **Roasted Cherry Tomato Confit** or even sweet fruits such as fresh peaches, ground cherries, or pears. It is an appropriate pairing with **Seeded Seaweed Snacking Crisps, Watermelon Jelly**, and fresh herbs.

Blushing Goat Spread

— MAKES ABOUT ¾ CUP —

This glowing, fuchsia-colored spread is more sweet than savory and receives enthusiastic reviews from everyone who tries it. The trick is using my secret weapon to add both sweetness and a rich, deep, fruit flavor: pomegranate molasses. Easily sourced at most Middle Eastern groceries, this is an ingredient to always keep on hand, and it blends beautifully with both bold, ruby fruits and earthy vegetables such as beets. (Recipe shown on page 40.)

55 g / ⅓ cup roasted beets, coarsely chopped
115 g / ½ cup goat cheese, softened
20 g / 1 tablespoon pomegranate molasses
3 g / 1 teaspoon orange zest
¼ teaspoon fine sea salt

20 g / 2 tablespoons dried plums or cranberries, finely chopped
20 g / 2 tablespoons toasted hazelnuts or pecans, chopped

Place the roasted beets in the bowl of a food processor and puree on high. Add the cheese, pomegranate molasses, zest, and salt, and process until smooth. Transfer the mixture to a piece of parchment paper and shape it into a ball or log. Wrap it tightly in plastic and chill in the refrigerator for at least 1 hour. Combine the chopped dried fruit and nuts on a plate or in a shallow bowl. When the cheese has stiffened, roll it in the chopped fruit and nuts to coat. Alternatively, you may transfer the cheese to a decorative jar and serve it sprinkled with the dried fruit and nuts.

TRY IT WITH . . . Serve smeared under a bed of **Spiced Plum Preserves**, or alongside **Cranberry, Apricot, and Apple Mostarda**. Take it in the savory direction by dressing with spring greens, such as pea shoots and sliced radishes, and garnishing with **Citrus Salt.** You may also simply drizzle it with honey and sprinkle with fresh pomegranate arils before serving.

Blue Cheese Spread

— SERVES 6 TO 8 —

This recipe is best made using a combination of blue cheeses to achieve a mild flavor with a chunky but spreadable consistency. My favorite hard blue from the South is a Kenney's Farmhouse cheese called Barren County Blue. Its firm texture and nutty undertones are a perfect pairing with the pine nuts. Whatever creamery you choose, quality artisanal ingredients will elevate this recipe to please even those who are skeptical of "stinky cheese."

---

115 g / ½ cup cream cheese, room temperature

45 g / ⅓ cup crumbled soft blue cheese,
    room temperature

¼ teaspoon fine sea salt

45 g / ⅓ cup crumbled hard blue cheese, cold

15 g / 1 tablespoon pine nuts, toasted and
    lightly chopped

25 g / 2 tablespoons finely minced red onion

½ tablespoon chopped fresh chives

In a small bowl, cream together the cream cheese, soft blue cheese, and salt using a spoon. Sprinkle in the rest of the ingredients and gently stir to combine, leaving crumbles of the hard blue cheese intact. Serve at room temperature. This spread will keep for up to 3 days in an airtight container in the refrigerator.

TRY IT WITH . . . This savory, nutty spread is delicious served on **Garlic Crostini** or **A Modest Baguette** topped with fresh fruit, such as pears, figs, or apples. When Concord grapes are in season, I like to toss a bunch in a little olive oil and chopped rosemary, roast in a 425°F oven until blistered and wrinkly, and serve them with this earthy treat. **Spiced Concord Grape Jam** is an excellent accompaniment as well.

Spicy Cheddar, Almond & Olive Ball

— SERVES 8 TO 10 —

If you are a child of the seventies, you may recognize that the most important ingredient in this recipe is nostalgia, as cheeseballs often bring to mind Tupperware parties in kitchens decorated in avocado green and harvest gold. Although these may not be your favorite colors, the retro cool of the cheeseball has solidly held its ground through recipe trends for good reason: their ingredients are adaptable, they can be made ahead of time, and they are a crowd pleaser at holiday gatherings. If you don't have slivered almonds on hand, chopped pistachios, pecans, or even pine nuts will marry nicely with the olives and pickled jalapeños. I prefer to use olives marinated in garlic and citrus zest, but plain green olives stuffed with pimientos work just as well. (Recipe shown on page 159.)

230 g / 1 cup cream cheese, room temperature

225 g / 2 cups extra sharp Cheddar cheese, grated

15 g / 1 tablespoon extra-virgin olive oil

1 teaspoon Citrus Salt (page 183)

45 g / ⅓ cup garlic-marinated green olives, pitted and chopped

30 g / 2½ tablespoons pickled jalapeños, drained and minced

⅔ cup slivered almonds, lightly toasted

Place the cream cheese, Cheddar, olive oil, and Citrus Salt in the bowl of a food processor. Blend on high until the mixture is creamy and consistent. Transfer the mixture to a small bowl and stir in the olives and jalapeños.

Place the almonds in a separate medium bowl. Using a spatula, transfer the cheese mixture to the bowl with the almonds, rolling to coat, and form it into a ball. Place the cheese ball on a serving dish and refrigerate for at least 1 hour before serving.

TRY IT WITH . . . **Sourdough Rye Crackers**, **Dipping Chips**, **Seeded Seaweed Snacking Crisps**, or **Garlic Crostini** are all excellent pairings for this party appetizer.

Preserved Lemon & Fava Bean Hummus

— MAKES ABOUT 3½ CUPS —

Fava beans are packed with protein, fiber, and iron and are a delicious alternative to chickpeas in this brightly flavored hummus. Just about any fresh herb will work well here, but I prefer mint, as it balances the earthy nuttiness of the favas. If you have the time, pop the beans out of their tough skins for a smoother-textured hummus. Or if you have a large mortar and pestle, you may prefer to make this by hand into a chunky spread rather than a smooth hummus. Both are delicious with their own particular character.

25 g / 3 plump garlic cloves, crushed and peeled

5 g / 1 teaspoon fine sea salt

½ teaspoon ground cumin

10 to 20 g / 1 to 2 tablespoons freshly squeezed lemon juice, to taste

425 g / 2½ cups cooked fava beans (see Kitchen Note)

120 g / ½ cup fava bean cooking liquid

110 g / ¼ cup Tahini Sauce (page 157)

5 to 10 g / 1 to 2 teaspoons Harissa (page 177)

70 g / ⅓ cup extra-virgin olive oil

45 g / 3 tablespoons rinsed and coarsely chopped Preserved Lemons (page 189)

2 tablespoons chopped fresh herbs

FOR THE GARNISH

15 g / 1 tablespoon extra-virgin olive oil

10 g / 1 tablespoon Dukkah (page 184)

1 teaspoon ground sumac

1 tablespoon chopped fresh herbs

Place the garlic, salt, cumin, and lemon juice in a food processor and pulse to form a paste. Add the beans, cooking liquid, tahini, and harissa and process on high, drizzling in the olive oil until smooth and creamy. (Don't worry if it seems a little thin—the hummus will thicken up after sitting.) Stir in the preserved lemon and chopped herbs and transfer to a serving bowl. Drizzle with olive oil and garnish with the dukkah, sumac, and additional chopped fresh herbs.

TRY IT WITH . . . This savory spread is excellent served with **Lavash**, **Spiced Carrot Levain**, **Miche**, **A Modest Baguette**, **Moonbread**, or **Garlic Crostini**. Serve with heaps of sprouts, fresh greens, or roasted or fresh vegetables.

KITCHEN NOTE Slow cooking is a convenient way to cook dried fava beans. Place 1 pound of dried beans in a large bowl and cover completely with water in excess of 3 inches. Soak the beans for 8 hours (or overnight). Rinse and drain the beans, sorting out and discarding any that look unsavory. Place them in your slow cooker with 2 bay leaves and cover with 6 cups of water. Stir in ¼ teaspoon of baking soda and cook on the low setting for about 8 to 9 hours or until the beans are soft and mashable with a fork.

Alternatively, you can use about 3 pounds of fresh, green fava beans as a substitution for dried. First you must shell the beans, then plunge them into boiling water to loosen their skins. Peel away the outer skin of each bean and transfer the beans to a deep saucepan. Pour in 3 cups of water and boil for about 30 minutes or until the beans are tender, adding a bit more water if necessary to prevent them from scorching.

Egg Salad

This recipe balances bright acidity with mellow creaminess to complement the crunch of the diced vegetables. Rainbow Relish (page 201) sets this egg salad apart from most others with a mellow background spice and a slight sweetness that makes for excellent picnic or lunch box fare. I prefer my egg salad to be more chopped than smooth, so you may wish to add 1 to 2 additional tablespoons of mayonnaise and/or mustard according to your preference.

55 g / ¼ cup Homemade Mayonnaise (page 180)

10 g / 2 teaspoons extra-virgin olive oil

1 teaspoon Fermented Grainy Mustard
    (page 179)

10 g / 1 tablespoon freshly squeezed lemon juice

About ¾ teaspoon fine sea salt, to taste

¼ teaspoon freshly ground black pepper

600 g / 12 large hard-boiled eggs, peeled
    and chopped

90 g / ¾ cup diced carrots

40 g / ¼ cup diced red bell pepper

35 g / ¼ cup finely sliced scallions

45 g / 2½ tablespoons drained Rainbow Relish
    (page 201)

1½ tablespoons chopped fresh herbs (parsley,
    basil, lovage, chives, cilantro, and/or dill)

Whisk together the mayonnaise, olive oil, mustard, lemon juice, salt, and pepper in a medium bowl. Stir in the remaining ingredients until well combined. This salad will keep for up to 3 days in an airtight container in the refrigerator.

TRY IT WITH . . . Serve on slices of **Miche** or **Pain de Mie** or on **Sourdough Whole-Grain Bagels** or **Pretzel Rolls**, with frilly mustard greens and sliced radishes, cherry tomatoes, or **Kraut**.

Herb Jam

Herb "jam" is a traditional recipe that is prepared in Morocco and was introduced to American kitchens by Paula Wolfert, the great cookbook author who inspired a new generation of Mediterranean cooking. This particular recipe's full-bodied, savory, herbal notes are balanced with the luminous contributions of Preserved Lemons (page 189) and vivid salty capers. The herb proportions are adaptable, and be sure to make use of any number of greens otherwise often neglected. My favorites to use are amaranth greens or radish tops! If using beneficial liver-cleansing bitter greens such as dandelion or chicory, taste for bitterness and mellow it out with another milder selection such as spinach.

---

60 to 75 g / 4 to 5 tablespoons extra-virgin olive oil

¾ teaspoon fine sea salt

40 g / 5 plump garlic cloves

1 teaspoon smoked paprika

½ teaspoon cayenne pepper (or to taste)

½ teaspoon ground cumin

455 g / 1 pound leafy greens (spinach, amaranth, arugula, beet, kale, dandelion, chicory, or radish greens work well)

25 g / 1 packed cup fresh cilantro leaves

25 g / 1 packed cup fresh parsley leaves

25 g / 1 packed cup fresh dill leaves

10 g / ½ cup fresh mint leaves

85 g / ½ cup rinsed and diced Preserved Lemons (page 189)

30 g / 2 tablespoons drained capers

In a large stock or preserving pot, toss 2 tablespoons of the oil with the spices, salt, garlic, and leafy greens. Place the pot over medium heat and cook for about 10 minutes or until the greens are completely wilted, stirring occasionally to encourage even cooking. Stir in the fresh herbs, preserved lemons, and capers and continue cooking until fragrant, about 5 more minutes.

Turn off the heat and use a slotted spoon to transfer the mixture to a chopping board, reserving the liquid for another use. Allow to cool slightly, then finely chop the mixture and transfer it to a lidded glass container. Drizzle the remaining olive oil over the mixture, adding more to cover if needed. Store in the refrigerator for up to 1 week. Serve at room temperature.

TRY IT WITH . . . Herb Jam is a wonderfully versatile condiment and can be stuffed into **Lavash** with hunks of Feta, oil-cured olives, and fresh tomatoes, or smeared on **Garlic Crostini** as an appetizer.

Crema de Carciofi
(Artichoke Cream)

— MAKES 1 CUP OR ½ PINT —

This is one of the simplest recipes you can prepare well in advance of serving. I keep some on hand at all times, as it is incredibly versatile and creamy yet contains no dairy. (Recipe shown on page 158.)

400 g / 1 packed cup canned artichoke hearts
    in water, very well drained
1 tablespoon chopped fresh basil or parsley leaves
25 g / about 3 plump garlic cloves

¾ teaspoon fine sea salt
½ teaspoon coarsely ground black pepper
75 g / ⅓ cup extra-virgin olive oil

Place the artichokes, basil, garlic, salt, and pepper in the bowl of a food processor. Process until the ingredients are fully combined and consistent. With the blade running, drizzle in the olive oil until a creamy, almost whipped texture is achieved (about 4 to 5 minutes), stopping to scrape down the sides of the bowl as necessary. Transfer into a serving dish and garnish with black pepper. Serve immediately or store in an airtight container in the refrigerator for up to 1 week.

TRY IT WITH . . . Spread it on a **Sourdough Whole-Grain Bagel**, a **Pretzel Roll**, or your favorite toast and top it with arugula, sliced in-season tomatoes, a drizzle of olive oil, and flaked sea salt. This versatile condiment is excellent with **Garlic Crostini**.

KITCHEN NOTE If you wish to make this spread when artichokes are at peak harvest, try using sautéed fresh artichoke hearts. First tear away the tough outer leaves of the fresh artichokes, lop off the tips, remove the fuzzy inner parts, and soak the remaining hearts in lemon water to discourage discoloration. Cook the hearts with a few tablespoons of oil, a generous squeeze of fresh lemon juice, and chopped fresh parsley until fork tender. Finely chop the cooked artichoke hearts with the remaining ingredients on a board instead of in a food processor. The results are completely different in texture but well worth the extra effort.

Ramp & Carrot Top Pesto Spread

— MAKES 2¼ CUPS OR ABOUT 1 PINT —

This savory, green recipe utilizes otherwise neglected carrot tops in combination with ramps, one of the most fleeting ingredients of spring. The result is a thick and mild, spreadable pesto excellent for any number of vegetable or meat pairings. If you prefer a more pronounced ramp flavor, simply skip the blanching process or blanch only one bunch of the ramps.

2,250 g / 10 cups water
250 g / 2 bunches ramps (about 40 small)
50 g / 1 bunch carrot tops
12 g / ½ cup fresh parsley leaves
80 g / ½ cup pistachios, toasted

25 g / ¼ cup grated pecorino cheese
¼ teaspoon freshly ground nutmeg
½ teaspoon coarsely ground black pepper
1¼ teaspoons Citrus Salt (page 183)
215 g / 1 cup extra-virgin olive oil

Bring the water to a boil in a large pot. Plunge the well-cleaned ramps and carrot tops into the water for about 30 seconds or until their color transforms to a deep, vibrant green. Immediately retrieve the greens with tongs and drain them in a colander.

Place the parsley, pistachios, and pecorino in the bowl of a food processor and pulse to combine. Add the blanched ramps and carrot tops along with the nutmeg, pepper, and salt, and pulse until everything is coarsely chopped and well combined. With the blade running on high, drizzle in the olive oil and continue processing until a thick, spreadable paste is formed. Transfer to a clean container and seal with plastic laid directly on top of the pesto to prevent discoloration. This will keep for up to 2 weeks in the refrigerator. Alternatively, leave out the cheese and freeze the pesto for up to 3 months.

TRY IT WITH . . . Use this pesto to generously adorn **Moonbread** or **Pretzel Rolls**, **A Modest Baguette**, or a crusty hearth loaf of your choice before dressing with **Sorghum-Roasted Carrots** or cured meat such as prosciutto. Garnish with fresh sprouts or crisp lettuce.

Garlic & Sun-Dried Tomato Confit

— MAKES ABOUT 1½ CUPS OR 1 PINT —

Confit is a term that refers to foods preserved in animal fat or oil, and it has long been used as a method to extend the shelf life of meats, vegetables, and also fruits. While garlic is a low-acid food that can be stored for extended periods if treated properly, I recommend preparing and eating this recipe within 1 to 2 weeks or using a pressure canner if you wish to preserve it for longer. Late spring through late summer is an excellent time to hunt for cured garlic at the market, depending on the variety and its cultivation requirements. You may also use whole unpeeled, plump seed heads that have been cured for added whimsy and flavor.

240 g / 4 to 5 heads garlic, cloves peeled

265 g / 1¼ cups extra-virgin olive oil

3 g / ½ teaspoon fine sea salt

½ teaspoon orange zest

2 large sprigs thyme

1 small sprig rosemary

40 g / ⅓ cup sun-dried tomatoes (optional)

Sterilize your jars according to the directions on page 20.

Place the garlic in a small saucepan and cover it with the oil. Stir in the salt, zest, and herbs and bring to a gentle simmer. Turn the heat to the lowest setting and poach the cloves for about 35 to 40 minutes or until soft but not falling apart. Gently stir in the tomatoes if using, and continue poaching for another 5 minutes or until the tomatoes are just soft.

Discard the herbs and use a slotted spoon to transfer the garlic and tomatoes to the drained, hot, sterilized jars. Pour in the oil to cover. Seal and allow to cool before placing in the refrigerator.

TRY IT WITH . . . Smear the tender and creamy garlic cloves onto **Dry Toast** and top with slivers of the sun-dried tomatoes, **Onion, Thyme, and Date Jam**, or add a dollop of **Lemony Herb Chèvre** or **Ricotta** for a savory **Garlic Crostini** perfect for entertaining.

S'chug

This Middle Eastern condiment, which originated in Yemeni cuisine, has a spicy kick and deep, herbal notes laced with the aromatic flavor of green cardamom seeds. Although it is traditionally made with just cilantro, I like to use a touch of mint, giving this pesto-like condiment a characteristic brightness. If you prefer to turn up the heat of this milder version, do not seed the chilies and use two or three jalapeños. (Recipe shown on page 158.)

70 g / 8 garlic cloves

10 g / 1 jalapeño pepper, seeded

3 large dried red chilies of your choosing,
    seeds removed

¼ teaspoon crushed green cardamom seeds

¼ teaspoon crushed whole cumin seeds

¼ teaspoon ground coriander

40 g / 1½ cups packed fresh cilantro leaves

10 g / ½ cup packed fresh mint leaves

5 g / 1½ teaspoons Citrus Salt (page 183)

230 g / ½ cup plus 1 tablespoon extra-virgin
    olive oil

Place everything but the oil in the bowl of a food processor and pulse until finely chopped and well combined. With the blade running, drizzle in the olive oil and continue processing until smooth (or according to preference). Taste and add more salt if needed, then transfer to a clean, covered container. Keep covered in the refrigerator for up to 2 weeks.

TRY IT WITH . . . Use S'chug to dress anything savory, including eggs, roasted or braised veggies, grilled meats such as skirt steak or lamb kebabs, hummus, or avocado. My favorite preparation is to mash half an avocado onto a piece of **Dry Toast**, drizzle generously with S'chug, layer with slices of watermelon radish, and sprinkle with **Dukkah** or black sesame seeds and Feta cheese.

Harissa

— MAKES 2 CUPS (450 G) OR 1 PINT —

While working at the Brooklyn Botanic Garden, I had a healthy competitive relationship with my Caribbean coworkers concerning homemade hot sauce. Every summer, the gardeners would grow a variety of peppers, only to result in a glut by September. We would share our fiery interpretations at the lunch table, and I learned a great deal about the different hot sauce–making traditions of each Caribbean island community. One thing was for sure: it had to have a mule kick of heat backed by a complexity of flavor.

Many of those peppers ended up dried and added to my already large collection of hot chilies. This sauce is influenced by the North African tradition of harissa paste, but with my own interpretation. You may use a variety of chilies, depending on your heat preference. I like to use a combination of pasilla or ancho chilies for their richness of flavor; puya or New Mexican chilies for their fruity complexity; a few chipotle or morita chilies for a smoldering, smoky note; kashmiri chilies for their mildness; and chiltepin or pequin chilies for their blast of heat. To take advantage of the seasons, try substituting fresh mango or persimmon pulp for the apples to balance the fire with a little sweetness. Carrots give the sauce some body, and there are several layers of acidity, including two forms of preserved citrus. Play with the flavors to your liking or availability, and taste to adjust along the way!

---

55 g / 2 ounces dried chilies

1 dried lime

105 g / ½ cup roasted red peppers

50 g / ⅓ cup peeled and coarsely chopped carrot

30 g / ¼ cup peeled and coarsely chopped apple of your choice

10 g / 1 tablespoon rinsed and chopped Preserved Lemons (page 189)

15 g / 2 plump garlic cloves

1 tablespoon chopped fresh cilantro

1 teaspoon coarsely chopped fresh mint

¾ teaspoon crushed cumin seeds, toasted

½ teaspoon crushed caraway seeds, toasted

¾ teaspoon ground coriander

¼ teaspoon ground cinnamon

30 g / 2 tablespoons extra-virgin olive oil

10 g / 1 tablespoon apple cider vinegar

10 g / 1 tablespoon freshly squeezed lemon juice

20 g / 1 tablespoon mild honey

About ½ teaspoon rose water, or more to taste

1 teaspoon orange zest

8 g / 1½ teaspoons fine sea salt

Sterilize your jars according to the directions on page 20.

Place the dried chilies in a heavy-bottomed skillet and toast them over medium-low heat for 5 to 7 minutes or until fragrant, stirring occasionally. Transfer the toasted chilies to a medium bowl, add the dried lime, and cover with boiling water. Cover the bowl with a plate and allow the chilies and dried lime to cool and soften for about 1½ hours. Drain the water and transfer the chilies and lime to the bowl of a food processor, along with the roasted red peppers, carrot, apple, preserved lemon, and garlic. Process on high until a thick paste forms. Add the remaining ingredients and continue to process until the sauce is thick and consistent.

Transfer the sauce to the drained, hot, sterilized jars and keep in the refrigerator for up to 6 months, where the flavors will infuse and grow more delicious with time.

TRY IT WITH . . . Harissa is one of the condiments I reach for most regularly to beat into scrambled eggs, mix into **Labneh**, **Preserved Lemon and Fava Bean Hummus**, or **Homemade Mayonnaise**. It is a key ingredient that lends a complex flavor to many recipes in this book.

Fermented Grainy Mustard

— MAKES A HEAPING ¾ CUP (200 G) OR ABOUT ½ PINT —

Homemade fermented mustards are ripe with healthy probiotics and rather easy to make, using up extra whey produced from straining yogurt or making Labneh (page 206). This is a basic recipe with a thick, dippable consistency and a slightly sweet flavor that becomes more acidic and pungent as it ages. Want a more exotic flavor? Feel free to add ½ tablespoon of chopped fresh tarragon, 1 teaspoon of grated fresh horseradish, a dash of bourbon, a little yogurt for creaminess, or even a tad more honey. You may enjoy it immediately after making or allow it to ferment for 1 to 2 days before storing the refrigerator. (Recipe shown on page 74.)

60 g / ⅓ cup yellow mustard seeds

25 g / 2 heaping tablespoons brown
 mustard seeds

8 g / 1 garlic clove, peeled and crushed

80 g / 6 tablespoons whey

20 g / 2 tablespoons apple cider vinegar (with
 the mother sediment for added probiotics)

20 g / 2 tablespoons freshly squeezed
 lemon juice

30 g / 1½ tablespoons mild honey

½ teaspoon ground turmeric

Combine the mustard seeds and garlic in the bowl of a food processor. Process on high to crack the seeds and chop the garlic, about 2 to 3 minutes. Add the remaining ingredients and continue processing on high until your desired consistency is achieved, scraping down the sides as necessary. (I prefer a balance between thick and grainy, about 6 to 7 minutes.)

Transfer the mustard into a clean jar with a tight-fitting lid, and allow it to ferment at room temperature for 1 to 2 days. The mustard will keep indefinitely in a sealed container in the refrigerator.

TRY IT WITH . . . Enjoy with **Soft Pretzels**, slathered on **The Best Grilled Cheese Sandwich**, or used as an ingredient in **Egg Salad**. It is excellent combined with **Onion, Thyme, and Date Jam** on an open-faced sandwich with sweet coppa.

Homemade Mayonnaise

— MAKES ABOUT 1 CUP OR ½ PINT —

This is a simple way to elevate the most humble ingredients into an affordable condiment, without scary industrial additives. The best way I have found to get the mayonnaise to thicken is to patiently whisk by hand, taking many breaks to relieve my forearm! You may use a quality blender or emulsion blender instead; the key to getting it emulsified is to slowly drizzle in the oil a little at a time, making sure it is fully incorporated before adding more. Customize the mayonnaise to suit your tastes, blitzing in a few cloves of black garlic if using a blender, adjusting the salt to preference, or even adding ¼ cup more oil if you like it less tangy.

Homemade mayonnaise is an excellent base for stirring in any number of enhancements to make a spreadable or dippable condiment for roasted or grilled veggies or meats. The variations below are a few simple suggestions to pique your imagination.

---

50 g / 3 large egg yolks

1½ teaspoons prepared smooth mustard
    (Dijon is my choice)

2 teaspoons freshly squeezed lemon juice

1 teaspoon apple cider vinegar

¼ teaspoon fine sea salt

160 g / ¾ cup vegetable oil

FOR GARLIC AIOLI

½ cup Homemade Mayonnaise

About 20 g / 2 tablespoons Garlic and
    Sun-Dried Tomato Confit (page 174),
    drained and mashed

10 g / 1 tablespoon freshly squeezed lemon juice

Pinch of fine sea salt

FOR SPICY AIOLI

½ cup Homemade Mayonnaise

30 g / 2 tablespoons rinsed and chopped
    Preserved Lemons (page 189), rinsed

8 g / 1½ teaspoons Harissa (page 177) or to taste

8 g / 1 plump garlic clove, minced

1 tablespoon chopped fresh mint

Pinch of fine sea salt

FOR CAPERED AIOLI

½ cup Homemade Mayonnaise

10 g / 1 tablespoon freshly squeezed lemon juice

5 g / 1 teaspoon Fermented Grainy Mustard
    (page 179)

1½ tablespoons chopped fresh herbs

8 g / 1 plump garlic clove, minced

Sprinkling of drained capers

Place the yolks, mustard, lemon juice, vinegar, and salt in a medium bowl and vigorously whisk until creamy. Slowly drizzle in the oil—first in drops, then increasing into a steady, slow stream to emulsify the yolk mixture. Continue whisking until the mayonnaise is thick and creamy. Taste and add more salt as desired, then transfer the mayonnaise to an airtight container and store it in the refrigerator for up to 2 weeks.

To make one of the flavor variations, vigorously stir all of the ingredients together in a small bowl. Cover and allow to chill in the refrigerator for at least 1 hour before serving. Flavored mayonnaises will keep in airtight containers in the refrigerator for up to 1 week.

TRY IT WITH . . . Homemade Mayonnaise is the perfect browning agent to use for **Mayonnaise Magic Skillet Toast** when preparing **The Best Grilled Cheese Sandwich**. Use it to elevate **Egg Salad** beyond the ho-hum. Make a simple and delicious condiment for Le Gran Aioli in the Provençal tradition, serving with crisp crudités and poached seafood.

SALT BLENDS

Salt blends using seasonal ingredients such as citrus zest or fresh herbs bring a surprising depth of flavor with just a flick of the fingers to otherwise simple meals. The following are two basic versions that will prove incredibly versatile for preparing recipes in this book or as a finishing salt at the table.

HERB SALT

If you are lucky enough to have a small patch of land or even a fire escape to cultivate a few herbs, this recipe will make it worth the effort. Make Herb Salt in late spring when you have an abundance of succulent nasturtium leaves, feathery fennel fronds, and fresh parsley at the ready. Toss in a handful of edible flowers, such as calendula, nasturtium, rose, marigold, lavender, or spicy mustard flowers, for a playful splotch of color. At the height of summer, when woody perennial herbs like rosemary, sage, and thyme contain the highest concentration of flavorful and aromatic oils, you can harvest them for this recipe and fill your kitchen with a wondrous fragrance that will last for days. I highly recommend that you take the time to process this recipe by hand, as the oils that are released will leave you relaxed and rejuvenated. Use Herb Salt as a replacement for regular salt in most savory recipes, sprinkle it over finished dishes, or bottle it and wrap it up nicely as gifts from your garden.

Toss 7 to 8 minced garlic cloves or ramp bulbs (optional) and 1 cup of salt together in a small bowl. Working in several batches, place 4 packed cups of herbs on a cutting board and coarsely chop. Sprinkle the salt and garlic mixture over the herbs and continue chopping until the mixture resembles coarse sand.

Alternatively, working in batches, place 2 cups of the herb leaves in the bowl of a food processor along with ¼ cup of salt. Pulse to a fine consistency and transfer to a medium bowl. Repeat this process and then combine with the remaining salt.

Spread the salt and herb mixture on a large sheet pan and place it in a well-ventilated location to dry for at least 5 days, depending on the moisture content of the herbs and the air. Transfer the salt mixture to clean, dry jars and store it in a cool, dry location for up to 6 months.

KITCHEN NOTE If using lavender leaves or flowers, just remember that this fragrant plant has a very powerful presence that can overwhelm the senses; use it only in small amounts in proportion to other herbs.

CITRUS SALT

This recipe is excellent for preserving the zest of citrus when you may be using only the juice of the fruit. I like to keep a small bowl on the counter, adding salt and zest in equal parts when convenient. You may also toss in other herbs or spices at your discretion, making flavorful mixes for your own kitchen or to gift for the holidays. Lavender and lemon, sage or rosemary and orange, and chili and lime are just a few combinations you might want to try.

Using a microplane, zest your fruit into a small bowl. Measure the zest and add equal parts salt and dried herbs (if using) to the bowl. Toss together to combine and leave uncovered on the counter for 1 to 2 days or until the zest feels dry to the touch. The salt will naturally pull the moisture from the zest, leaving behind the fragrant oils in concentration. Crush the mixture with your fingers to break up the dried zest, transfer the mixture to clean, dry jars, and store in a cool, dry place for up to 1 year.

KITCHEN NOTE If a recipe calls for Citrus Salt and you don't have any prepared, simply substitute with equal parts fresh zest and salt.

Dukkah

I first discovered this exotic and aromatic blend in a South African specialty foods store. It quickly became my favorite popcorn flavoring before I learned of its potential as a dipping or finishing spice for bread. I always keep a homemade version of it on hand, as it easily dresses up a quick lunch or morning breakfast routine. Its contents reflect a versatile combination of whole toasted seeds and nuts and various dried herbs. I like to include a sprinkling of dried flowers—especially hibiscus petals—for a bright, zingy, decorative finish. Choose from pine nuts, hazelnuts, pumpkin seeds, pistachios, or almonds and adjust the spices to your preference. The following is one of my favorite blends, but I encourage you to play and experiment with what your garden and pantry provide! (Recipe shown on page 166.)

---

80 g / ½ cup raw unsalted pepitas

70 g / ½ cup raw unsalted hazelnuts

1 small dried chili of your choice

50 g / ⅓ cup black sesame seeds

1 teaspoon cumin seeds

1 teaspoon fenugreek seeds

1 teaspoon nigella (black cumin) seeds

1 whole dried mace blade

¾ teaspoon whole black peppercorns or
grains of paradise

1 teaspoon dried lavender petals

2 tablespoons dried hibiscus flowers

1 teaspoon dried thyme

½ teaspoon dried marjoram

1 teaspoon ground sumac

1 tablespoon dried rose, pineapple sage,
or calendula flowers

2 teaspoons Citrus Salt (page 183)

Preheat your oven to 350°F. Spread the pepitas and hazelnuts in separate groups on a sheet pan and place it in the oven. Check the color of the pepitas after 8 to 9 minutes, as they will be done before the hazelnuts. When the pepitas are toasted to your liking, transfer them to a plate to cool, stir the hazelnuts, and return the sheet pan to the oven. Continue toasting the hazelnuts for another 3 to 5 minutes or until their skins begin to curl. Remove the sheet pan from the oven and set it aside to cool. When the hazelnuts are cool enough to handle, rub them in a kitchen towel to release their skins.

Place the dried chili; sesame, cumin, fenugreek, and nigella seeds; mace; and black peppercorns in a large, heavy-bottomed skillet. Toast over medium-low heat for 5 to 7 minutes or until fragrant. Allow to cool and transfer about three quarters of the toasted seeds and spices to the bowl of a food processor along with three quarters of the toasted hazelnuts and pepitas. Add the lavender and hibiscus and pulse to grind into a semi-fine seasoning, being careful not to overprocess. Place the remaining toasted spices and nuts in a mortar and grind them with a pestle to form a coarse seasoning. Transfer both mixtures to a small bowl along with the remaining ingredients, and stir to combine. Store the spice blend in a clean, airtight container in a cool, dark place for up to 1 month. Alternatively, store it in an airtight container in the freezer for up to 3 months.

TRY IT WITH . . . Serve as a dipping spice with **Miche**, **A Modest Baguette**, **Moonbread**, or **Spiced Carrot Levain** alongside a bowl of fine-quality extra-virgin olive oil. Sprinkle over **Labneh** and smear onto a slice of **Skillet Toast** or **Dry Toast**, or reach for **Dukkah** to easily make avocado toast way more interesting and flavorful! It is an excellent finishing spice for the tartine toppers in chapter 7, especially the **Grilled Escarole**, **Sorghum-Roasted Carrots**, or **Pan-Fried Cauliflower in Curried Yogurt Marinade**.

> **KITCHEN NOTE** Drying edible flower petals when they are in season gives you an excellent opportunity to add a flourish of color, texture, and flavor to dishes at any time of the year. Simply cut the flowers, leaving about a 6-inch stem, bind them with twine, and hang them upside-down in a well-ventilated area until dry, separating the petals from the stems before storing. Alternatively, remove the petals from the stems and separate them onto a clean, porous paper– or parchment-lined sheet pan. Place in a well-ventilated area and allow to dehydrate naturally for at least 1 week until completely dry. Store in clean, dry containers for up to 6 months.

6

Ferments, Pickles & Cured Ingredients

METHODS OF PRESERVATION extend exponentially beyond this book, but included in this chapter are some of my favorite examples of accoutrements and cured ingredients that boost and brighten any meal. The time required and ingredients vary, but you need not have any special technical skills other than the ability to read the recipe. Salt plays a particularly important role in the success of these recipes, and it is important to use quality ingredients. If you approach these methods with an open mind and a thirst for experimentation, you will be surprised by the palette of flavors not easily found readymade.

◄ *Top, left to right:* Beet-Cured Gravlax, Kraut. *Bottom, left to right:* Sourdough Whole-Grain Bagels, Quickles, Lemony Herb Chèvre, Baccalà Mantecato.

Preserved Lemons

— MAKES ONE LARGE 1-LITER JAR OR 2 PINTS —

Winter is high season for Meyer lemons, my favorite citrus to use in a variety of dishes rang-
ing from sweet to savory. Their perfumed thin skins and complex flavor can be enjoyed fresh
for only a short time, making them the perfect seasonal candidates for preservation. I prefer
to make one neutral jar of preserved lemons without spice and several laced with aromatic
flavors that remind me of navigating the exotic souks of the medina quarter of Marrakesh.

The following recipe can be adapted using other citrus as well: try common Eureka lemons, limes, clementines, or mandarins. Just be sure to use organic citrus to avoid the cocktail
of sprays that most conventional fruits endure. The thinner the skin, the more likely you
will want to quarter the fruit before salting. If using thick-skinned fruits, such as common
lemons, limes, or oranges, you may slice them into ½-inch-thick rounds before salting and
stacking them into jars slightly larger than the width of the fruit.

---

800 g / 8 to 9 small Meyer lemons

240 g / 1 cup coarse sea salt

75 to 110 g / ⅓ to ½ cup freshly squeezed
    lemon juice, as needed

OPTIONAL SPICES

3 whole cloves

1½ tablespoons candied ginger, coarsely chopped

1 cinnamon stick

1 star anise pod

or

3 whole bay leaves

1 teaspoon whole coriander seeds

Sprinkle about ¼ inch of salt in the bottom of the jar. Set aside.

Quarter the lemons three-fourths of the way down, leaving one end intact, or slice the
lemons into rounds. Remove any seeds and place the fruit pieces in a large bowl. Stuff the
quartered lemons with a few pinches of salt. Toss the citrus with the remaining salt and allow
them to sit at room temperature for about 10 minutes.

Lightly press down on the fruit to extract the juice, then pack it into the jar, alternating
layers with the spices (if using). Pour in the remaining juice from the bowl. Add enough
squeezed lemon juice to completely cover the salted lemons. Position the lid to seal and
place the jar in a cool, dry location, tamping it lightly to eliminate any trapped air. Leave the
jar for at least 1 month to cure.

To use, simply remove the slices or wedges from their brining jar and rinse them. Screw the lid back on the jar and store the remaining lemons in a cool location or in the refrigerator for up to 1 year.

TRY IT WITH . . . Use to brighten **Preserved Lemon and Fava Bean Hummus**, swirl into **Labneh**, or add a surprising complexity to an aioli made with **Homemade Mayonnaise**. It is a signature ingredient in the savory **Herb Jam** and is kismet for the **Warm Brussels Sprouts Salad**.

KITCHEN NOTE If the lemons float to the top of the brine, you will need to weight them to keep them from being exposed to air.

Quickles

Quick pickling (or quickling, if you want to say it as speedily as you make it) is an easy way to use a glut of produce, and it doesn't require any special canning equipment. An array of vegetables can be used by themselves or in colorful combination. The spices may also be adjusted according to which fruits and vegetables you choose: just be mindful of how their flavors may influence each other. The amount of liquid needed will fluctuate according to how you slice, dice, or julienne your choices, but the following is a general guide for a 1-quart jar.

455 g / 1 pound mixed vegetables

Spices and seasonings of your choice (see right)

8 to 15 g / 1 to 2 plump garlic cloves, peeled and halved

225 g / 1 cup white vinegar

225 g / 1 cup water

20 g / 1 tablespoon mild honey or granulated sugar

10 g / 2 teaspoons fine sea salt

OPTIONAL (CHOOSE YOUR PREFERRED COMBINATION, INSPIRED BY THE FOLLOWING):

Beets and/or purple carrots with 1 cinnamon stick; 4 or 5 whole cloves; 1 teaspoon cumin, caraway, and/or coriander seeds; and a fresh or dried chili

Green beans or sliced cucumbers with 1 to 3 sprigs fresh dill and a handful of garlic scapes

Peeled broccoli stems and/or kohlrabi with 1½ teaspoons black peppercorns crushed with a mortar and pestle

Daikon radish with a 1-inch piece sliced fresh ginger and/or galangal and ½ of a small shaved turmeric root

Breakfast radishes with cilantro and/or coriander seeds

Wild spring onion bulbs with spruce or juniper tips

Ripe white or slightly under-ripe red strawberries with a few cardamom pods

Slice, julienne, or mandoline the veggies to a uniform thickness. Place the spices in the bottom of one sterilized quart-size jar or two sterilized pint-size jars (see page 20). Make a slit in the side of the hot pepper, if using. Pack the veggies and garlic in the jar.

Place the vinegar, water, sweetener, and salt in a small saucepan and heat over medium low, stirring occasionally to create a brine. When the sweetener and salt have fully dissolved, pour the hot liquid over the packed veggies. Allow the pickles to brine for at least 2 hours before serving. The longer they brine, the more saturated and intense the seasonings will be. Keep the pickles in their tightly sealed jars for up to 3 months in the refrigerator.

TRY IT WITH . . . Excellent on sandwiches, chopped into savory chicken or egg salads, or served alongside a cheese or charcuterie plate, these pickles add a punch of flavor to any meal.

KITCHEN NOTE If you eat your pickles within a few weeks, you can reuse the brine in a cold pickling process, adding more vegetables or tender fruits, such as blackberries, to the jar. The brine is also wonderful mixed into salad dressings.

Fermented Brined Pickles

— MAKES 4 CUPS, 1 QUART, OR 2 PINTS —

There isn't much you need regarding time or resources to ferment fresh vegetables. The result is a somewhat sour "pickle" packed with an increased amount of vitamins and beneficial microbial populations. I hesitate to even offer a recipe, as the method is really more about proportion than specific ingredients. Roughly speaking, I use a brine of 2–3% salt to weight of the water, making it essential to own a scale if you want to ferment large batches. This yields a pickle high in healthful lactic acid bacteria, but it tastes only slightly salty. A 2–3% brine is not suitable for canning, as it will not yield a pickle with high enough acidity. If you wish to make a fully sour pickle for canning, simply use a 5% salt solution instead.

Like with the other pickled recipes in this book, your imagination is your only limitation for seasoning, with the following as a rough guideline. If you're not sure where to start, try 1 cup each of peeled and chopped kohlrabi, apples, daikon, and carrots; a 1-inch piece of fresh ginger, sliced; 5 sprigs of fresh cilantro; and 2 cloves of crushed garlic. Before getting started, please read the section about fermentation on page 23 for helpful hints on appropriate jars, weights, and temperatures.

Spices and seasonings of choice
(see Quickles on page 191 for suggestions)
455 g / 1 pound fresh vegetables, trimmed and
cut to preference

11 g / 2 heaping teaspoons fine sea salt
450 g / 2 cups water

Place the spices and seasonings in a jar or jars large enough to accommodate your method of weighting (see page 24). Arrange your vegetables in the jar, packing them as tightly as you can.

In a medium bowl, stir the salt into the water until it is completely dissolved. It will first appear cloudy and will then clear up again before it's ready. Pour the brine over the vegetables, weighting them down to keep them submerged. Seal and place the jar(s) in an undisturbed location.

After about 3 days, you will see and smell fermentation activity. When foam rises to the surface, skim and discard it before weighting again. The vegetables generally take about 5 to 14 days to ferment before they're ready to be refrigerated. Taste as you go and store the fermented pickles in the refrigerator when they have reached your desired flavor, keeping in mind that they will continue to ferment, albeit at a much slower rate.

TRY IT WITH . . . These are fantastic served with **Baccalà Mantecato** on toasted **Black Bread**, **Miche**, or **Spiced Carrot Levain**. Although their color somewhat dulls and clouds a bit with extended fermentation time, they make for a unique presentation and flavor profile on a cheese or charcuterie board.

KITCHEN NOTE I have found that the washed and clean ends of root vegetables or green onions can help encourage an active fermentation culture. If you don't want to eat these ends, trim and reserve them to dress the top of the brine, discarding them before eating if they develop any scum. Likewise, using the leaves of vegetables like radishes or beets in both the bottom and top of the jar provides an excellent opportunity for the beneficial bacteria present on the leaves to thrive, resulting in a healthy and delicious pickle.

Kraut

When vegetables are mixed with salt, their natural juices are extracted in an osmotic process, creating their own brine. We further massage these to encourage more liquid release before the vegetables are packed into jars, weighted, and left to ferment at room temperature. The continued presence of salt acts to regulate the fermentation process from this point forward, taking anywhere from 5 to 14 days to reach a pleasant, sour flavor. Please refer to page 24 for more tips on proper jars, weights, and methods for successful vegetable fermentation.

This kraut recipe and the kimchi recipe that follows are two versions of the same process. They are meant to act as practice or "gateway" recipes if you are new to fermenting. With time, you will feel more comfortable adjusting the ingredients to suit your preferences, with only your imagination limiting the possibilities.

One of my closest friends insists that sauerkraut includes nothing other than cabbage, either red or green. I prefer to add a few spices to lace it with a piney, caraway flavor, but these are completely optional. You may also go bold and substitute other vegetables into the mix, such as carrots, apples, kohlrabi, or onions, keeping the salt content at 2% or 3% of the total vegetable weight. Just be aware that you may be scolded by any Bavarians who hear you describe a nontraditional ferment as sauerkraut!

---

720 g / about 1 small head red cabbage, cored and sliced ¼ inch thick

18 g / 3½ teaspoons fine sea salt

½ teaspoon caraway seeds (optional)

3 juniper berries, lightly crushed with a mortar and pestle (optional)

Place the cabbage in a large bowl and sprinkle it with the remaining ingredients. With your hands or a kraut tamper, squeeze or pound the mixture until it releases its juices and becomes somewhat watery, about 10 to 12 minutes. Continue until the juices are able to cover the cabbage when you gently tamp it down.

Transfer the cabbage to a quart-size mason jar or a crock that is large enough to accommodate the volume and weight, pour in enough of the juices to cover completely, and weight the vegetables down. Seal the jar or container and set it aside in a moderately warm location (about 75°F); allow to ferment for about 5 to 14 days, checking periodically. If any scum forms on the surface, simply remove the top layer of vegetables, weight the remaining vegetables down once more, and continue fermenting. When the mixture has reached your desired level of taste, move it to the refrigerator for storage. It will keep for up to 1 year, increasing in complexity of flavor with time.

TRY IT WITH . . . This is one of my favorite toppings for just about any savory sandwich or tartine, especially made with **Sourdough Whole-Grain Bagels**, **Pretzel Rolls**, **Buttermilk Rye**, **Miche**, **Black Bread**, **or Spiced Carrot Levain**. It goes especially well with **Baccalà Mantecato** and **Egg Salad**, and it makes any prepared egg look especially desirable.

Kimchi

— MAKES ABOUT 2 QUARTS —

The salty, umami goodness of Korean kimchi is traditionally flavored with fish sauce. Generally in dry-salt ferments, I use an amount of salt equal to 2–3% of the total vegetable weight, but less salt is used in this kimchi recipe in consideration of the fish sauce. If you wish to make a vegan version, adjust the salt accordingly. For a few variations, substitute apples or pears for part of the radishes, green beans for some of the carrots, or in-season garlic scapes for the garlic cloves. Just be sure to keep the weight to salt ratio about the same, weighing the total ingredients before adjusting and adding the salt. In traditional kimchi recipes, Korean red pepper flakes (gochugaru) would be used, but you may substitute with any hot, fruity dried ground pepper such as Kashmiri or puya. Go easy with the spices at first and add more to taste.

1250 g / 12½ packed cups sliced napa cabbage
    (1- to 2-inch-thick slices)
280 g / 2 cups sliced radishes
240 g / 2 cups peeled and sliced carrots
50 g / 3 whole scallions, trimmed and cut into
    1-inch pieces
40 g / 4-inch piece fresh ginger, peeled
    and grated

25 g / 3 plump garlic cloves
1 to 3 tablespoons red pepper flakes
40 g / 4 tablespoons fish sauce
    (no preservatives added)
30 g / 2 tablespoons fine sea salt
20 g / 1 tablespoon mild honey

Combine the cabbage, radishes, carrots, and scallions in a large bowl. In the bowl of a food processor (or with a large mortar and pestle), grind the ginger, garlic, red pepper flakes, and fish sauce to a smooth paste. Transfer the paste to the bowl of vegetables and add the salt and honey. With gloved hands or a kraut tamper, squeeze or pound the mixture until it releases its juices and becomes somewhat watery, about 10 to 12 minutes. Continue until the juices are able to cover the vegetables when they are gently tamped down, taking breaks as needed.

Transfer the vegetables and juices to two quart-size mason jars or other crocks large enough to accommodate the volume and weight. Weight down the vegetables in each jar until they are completely submerged in brine. Seal and set the jars aside (in a sequestered location if you are sensitive to strong smells); allow the kimchi to ferment for about 7 to 10 days, checking periodically. If any scum forms on the surface, simply remove the top layer of vegetables, weigh the remaining vegetables once more, and continue fermenting.

When the mixture has reached your desired level of taste, move it to the refrigerator for storage. It will keep for up to 1 year, increasing in complexity of flavor with time.

TRY IT WITH . . . Kimchi is excellent served on a tartine with a boiled or fried egg or pulled pork. Use it as a substitute for **Rainbow Relish** in **Egg Salad**, to spice up **The Best Grilled Cheese Sandwich**, or to add an extra punch of flavor to **Preserved Lemon and Fava Bean Hummus**. Nibble with **Seeded Seaweed Snacking Crisps** for a spicy treat.

Rainbow Relish

This recipe was developed as a result of having just a little too much zucchini on hand! Employing a menagerie of colorful chopped and shredded veggies and inspired pickling spices, this deliciously sweet and sour condiment is not unlike the chow-chow relish I grew up with in the South. (Recipe shown on page 158.)

1050 g / 2 to 3 zucchini, shredded (8 cups)

260 g / about 6 medium purple carrots, peeled and chopped (2 cups)

375 g / 1 large red onion, chopped (2½ cups)

500 g / 3 cups fresh corn kernels (from about 4 ears)

375 g / about 2 medium red bell peppers, finely chopped (2½ cups)

150 g / 1 medium yellow bell pepper, finely chopped (1 cup)

150 g / 1 large purple or green bell pepper, finely chopped (1 cup)

220 g / 2 cups finely chopped red Swiss chard stems (from 1 large bunch)

135 g / ½ cup fine sea salt

790 g / 3½ cups apple cider vinegar

225 g / 1 cup water

340 g / 1 cup mild honey

200 g / 1 cup raw sugar

2 teaspoons whole fenugreek seeds

1 teaspoon ground turmeric

2 teaspoons whole cumin seeds

2 teaspoons whole mustard seeds

2 teaspoons whole coriander seeds

2 teaspoons red pepper flakes

½ to 2 habanero peppers with seeds, finely minced

Sterilize your jars according to the directions on page 20.

Place the veggies in a large bowl and toss them with the salt. Cover the bowl and let it sit for 1 hour, allowing the juices to develop.

Meanwhile, combine the vinegar, water, honey, sugar, and spices in a large pot. Bring the mixture to a boil over high heat and cook for 5 minutes. Turn off the heat and allow the brine to infuse for at least 30 minutes.

Squeeze as much liquid as you can from the vegetables and place them in a clean bowl. Strain the brine through a fine-mesh sieve into the bowl with the vegetables and stir to combine. Pack the vegetable and brine mixture into the sterilized jars, pouring in enough liquid to cover the vegetables completely. Position the lids and rings and heat process the jars for 10 minutes according to instructions on page 22.

FERMENTS, PICKLES & CURED INGREDIENTS

TRY IT WITH . . . Traditionally served with cornbread and a pot of pinto beans laced with a ham hock, this relish goes wonderfully well on a tartine accompanied by **Preserved Lemon and Fava Bean Hummus**. It is also excellent mixed into cream cheese for **Sourdough Whole-Grain Bagels** or used in **Egg Salad**. Enjoy simply served on **Seeded Seaweed Snacking Crisps** or **Sourdough Rye Crackers**.

Cardamom Pickled Watermelon Rind

— MAKES 2 QUARTS —

I like preparing Watermelon Jelly (page 114) and this recipe within the same weekend, as you can make use of almost the whole melon with minimal food waste. These sweet and sour pickles pack a spicy kick and a bit of heat. Be sure to rinse them well after the overnight soak to prevent them from becoming too salty upon processing. You may use dried smoky chilies instead of fresh hot peppers if you wish, placing them in the pot while preparing the brine.

FOR THE PICKLES

1,130 g / 5 cups water (100°F)
90 g / ⅓ cup fine sea salt
740 g / 6 cups chopped watermelon rind
   (see Kitchen Note)
6 green cardamom pods, split
2 teaspoons whole coriander seeds,
   lightly crushed with a mortar and pestle
2 teaspoons whole pink peppercorns,
   lightly crushed with a mortar and pestle
60 g / 1 small lime, thinly sliced
15 g / 2 plump garlic cloves, peeled and halved
1-inch piece fresh ginger, peeled and sliced
2 to 3 fresh chilies of your choice, halved with
   seeds (habanero, jalapeño, etc.)

FOR THE BRINE

340 g / 1½ cups water
280 g / 1¼ cups white or rice vinegar
170 g / ½ cup mild honey
8 g / 1½ teaspoons fine sea salt

In a large bowl, stir together the water and salt until the salt is completely dissolved. Transfer the chopped watermelon rind to the bowl; cover and refrigerate for 6 to 12 hours.

Sterilize your jars according to the directions on page 20.

Rinse the watermelon rind under cold running water and drain it well in a colander. In a large saucepan, prepare the brine by stirring together the water, vinegar, honey, and salt. Bring the mixture to a boil over high heat, add the drained watermelon rind to the pot, and return the mixture to a boil. Cook for about 5 minutes, skimming off any foam that may form on the surface.

Sprinkle in a few teaspoons of the spices in the bottom of each hot, drained, sterilized jar. Remove the pot from the heat and use a ladle to pack the watermelon rind into the jars, alternating with the lime, garlic, ginger, chilies, and remaining spices. Pour the brine into the jars, leaving about ¼ inch of headspace. Run a clean spoon down the side of the jars to release any trapped air bubbles. Position the lids and cool to room temperature. Store the watermelon pickles in sealed jars in the refrigerator for up to 3 months.

TRY IT WITH . . . This unusual addition is a delightful surprise on a pickle plate and one that always gets puzzled but pleased responses from anyone who didn't grow up eating them in the South! Finely chop and add these pickles to chicken salad, serve alongside a grilled burger, or add to a cheese plate.

KITCHEN NOTE To prepare the rind, cut away the inner red flesh for eating or making into Watermelon Jelly (page 114). Use a vegetable peeler to remove the green outer skin, and cut the white flesh into consistently sized chunks, about 1 inch or to your preference. If you prefer a fancier pickle, try cutting them into fun shapes using a fluted knife or small cookie cutter.

Labneh

— MAKES ABOUT 1 CUP YOGURT CHEESE AND ABOUT 1 CUP WHEY —

The process of making labneh yields two ingredient gifts in one: a wonderful, spreadable yogurt cheese that can be spiked with an infinite choice of fresh flavors, and a bioactive and beneficial whey by-product. Whey is an underused ingredient with a myriad of potential uses. It is a wonderful fermentation and flavor booster for juices and smoothies, and it is a standard ingredient in Fermented Grainy Mustard (page 179). You can also use it as a sub-stitution for water to hydrate bread dough, resulting in a softer, tenderer crumb. Try it in combination with the carrot juice in Spiced Carrot Levain (page 45) or Miche (page 33). (Recipe shown on page 102.)

FOR THE LABNEH
455 g / 2 cups plain whole-milk yogurt,
    stirred well

FOR ROSE-SCENTED LABNEH
1½ tablespoons mild honey
¾ teaspoon rose water (or to taste)

FOR SWEETENED AND PINK LABNEH
1½ tablespoons mild honey
1 teaspoon beet root powder

FOR SWEETENED AND GREEN LABNEH
1½ tablespoons mild honey
1 teaspoon matcha powder

FOR MINTY LABNEH
½ tablespoon dried or 1 tablespoon chopped
    fresh mint

FOR GARLICKY LABNEH
1 garlic clove, minced

FOR SPICED LABNEH
1 tablespoon zaatar or Dukkah (page 184)
1 teaspoon minced fresh ginger

FOR THE GARNISHES, TRY ONE OR A COMBINATION OF THE FOLLOWING:
Chopped toasted pistachios or pine nuts
Fresh or dried herbs
Fresh or dried rose petals
Rinsed and diced Preserved Lemons (page 189)
Extra-virgin olive oil

At least 1 day in advance of intended use, completely wet and wring dry a cheesecloth. Line the top of a deep container with the cheesecloth and secure it with a rubber band, allowing the cloth to droop and form a cradle but not touch the bottom of the container, with at least 4 inches of room in the bottom. Spoon the yogurt into the cheesecloth, cover the container, and allow it to drain overnight or longer in the refrigerator. (The longer you leave it to drain, the thicker the consistency will be.) The whey will collect in the bottom of the container, and you will be left with a thick, spreadable cheese in the cloth. Use it as is or combine with your preferred flavorings to make savory or sweet variations.

TRY IT WITH . . . My favorite way to use plain or savory Labneh is smeared onto just about any **Dry Toast** or **Skillet Toast** and topped with slices of avocado or **Pickled Shrimp**, dusted with **Dukkah**, and served alongside a soft-boiled egg and **Fermented Brined Pickles** or **Quickles**.

It is also delicious sweetened and generously spooned onto **Baked Pain Perdu**, topped with fresh fruits such as plump figs, sun-ripened strawberries, or juicy sliced peaches. Dust with edible flowers for a beautiful presentation, or finish with a dollop of **Strawberry and Meyer Lemon Preserves** or **Violet Petal Jam**.

Crème Fraîche

This rich and slightly sour thickened cream is one of the easiest cultures to attempt and will leave you wondering why you ever paid such outrageously high prices for a small container at specialty groceries. I have had better luck using whole-milk yogurt to inoculate the cream, but good, farm-fresh buttermilk will work well, too. If you can source cream that is not ultra-pasteurized, you will have greater luck culturing the microbes that make this recipe a success. (Clotted cream variation shown on page 79.)

---

240 g / 1 cup heavy cream

45 g / 3 tablespoons whole-milk buttermilk or plain whole-milk yogurt

Place the heavy cream in a small bowl and whisk in the buttermilk or yogurt. Cover with a clean towel or cheesecloth and place in a warm spot such as on top of the refrigerator for 6 to 24 hours, depending on the ambient temperature of your kitchen. When it has reached a spoonable consistency, cover the mixture with plastic and store it in the refrigerator for up to 2 weeks, where it will continue to thicken.

TRY IT WITH . . . The French prefer it as their cream of choice for sauces, and once you taste it, you will know why. Its thick, custard-like texture resists curdling and has the body to be served drizzled with **Infused Honey**, stirred into **Horseradish Apple Cream**, or used in place of milk to make **Currant Cream Scones** a bit more succulent and moist. It is brilliant as a foil to cold-smoked trout roe, paired with **Black Bread**, **Miche**, **Buttermilk Rye**, or **Sourdough Whole-Grain Bagels**.

To make your own Clotted Cream to serve with scones, simply whip up 1 cup (240 g) of heavy cream and gently fold in ⅓ cup (70 g) of Crème Fraîche and about 1 tablespoon of powdered sugar or honey.

Horseradish Apple Cream

— MAKES ABOUT 1¾ CUPS —

Decadently creamy with a sweet but pungent flavor, this Polish spread is a delightful accompaniment to smoked fish or meats. If you don't have crème fraîche on hand, simply substitute with sour cream. (Recipe shown on page 212.)

75 g / ¾ cup grated green tart apple
   (about 1 small apple)
5 g / 1 teaspoon fine sea salt
210 g / 1 cup Crème Fraîche (page 208)

20 g / 3 teaspoons prepared or grated
   fresh horseradish
½ teaspoon lemon zest
Freshly ground black pepper, to taste

In a small bowl, stir together the apple and salt. Cover and allow to sit for about 20 to 30 minutes at room temperature. The salt will draw the water from the grated apples. Rinse and drain the apples in a colander, squeezing out any excess moisture. Place the drained apples in a clean, airtight container and combine them with the remaining ingredients. Cover and refrigerate for at least 30 minutes before serving. It will keep covered in the refrigerator for up to 3 days.

TRY IT WITH . . . Use to accompany smoked fish, sausages, roast beef, or soft-boiled eggs. Spread it onto **Black Bread**, **Buttermilk Rye**, **Sourdough Whole-Grain Bagels**, or **Pretzel Rolls** and top with **Baccalà Mantecato** and/or shaved fennel and dill.

Ricotta

— MAKES ABOUT 2 CUPS (500 G) —

Served warm straight from the strainer or mixed with seasonal flavors, these delicate curds are an irresistible treat that require just a few quality ingredients and very little time. As with Crème Fraîche (page 208), be sure to source full-fat milk and cream that are not ultra-pasteurized, or the mixture will not curdle. You can use lemon juice or vinegar as an acidifier—whichever you have on hand!

1,430 g / 6 cups whole milk

460 g / 2 cups heavy cream

5 g / 1 teaspoon fine sea salt

65 g / 6 tablespoons freshly squeezed lemon juice or white wine vinegar

Set a fine-mesh sieve over a large bowl and line the sieve with cheesecloth or a jelly bag.

Pour the milk and cream into a large, heavy-bottomed pot and stir in the salt. Bring the mixture to just under a boil (a thermometer should read 190°F to 200°F) and stir in the lemon juice. Turn off the heat and allow the mixture to sit for about 30 minutes until it visibly curdles and the thick, cheesy curds separate from the watery whey.

Pour the mixture into the lined sieve and allow it to drain at room temperature for 1 hour, or cover and refrigerate for up to 36 hours. The longer it drains, the dryer the ricotta will be—about 30 minutes yields a very soft ricotta, several days for a firm cheese. If it becomes too dry, simply stir a bit of the whey back into the curds. Serve immediately or store covered in the refrigerator for up to 1 week.

TRY IT WITH . . . Ricotta's uniquely versatile, creamy decadence can be served sweet or savory. Try mixing in a little lemon zest and chopped herbs and serving with **Roasted Cherry Tomato Confit**. Fortify your toast with this ricotta before topping with the jam of your choosing. It is also excellent drizzled with a little **Infused Honey** or topped with fresh seasonal fruits or **Honey-Roasted Rhubarb Compote**.

KITCHEN NOTE If you want to add a little seasonal flair, try steeping fresh or dried flower petals in the milk while it is heating. Two teaspoons of dried lavender or marigold or 1½ tablespoons of calendula or hibiscus lends an array of beautiful colors and subtle flavors to your ricotta. I prefer to put these into a tea strainer to steep, removing the strainer before adding the lemon juice, but you may add them loose if you don't mind the texture in the ricotta.

Beet-Cured Gravlax

— MAKES 1 LARGE SALMON FILLET —

This salmon is a balanced expression of deep, savory spices and an earthy-sweet beet identity. It makes an utterly stunning display, and it is one of my favorite things to serve during the holidays. It requires about three days to cure but is simple to plate once it is ready. I love using panela for its rich caramel sweetness but if you cannot source it, substitute with muscovado or brown sugar instead.

140 g / ½ cup fine sea salt

65 g / ½ cup coarsely grated panela

6 g / 2 teaspoons orange zest

½ tablespoon coarsely ground black pepper

1 teaspoon juniper berries, crushed with
   a mortar and pestle

½ teaspoon caraway seeds, crushed with
   a mortar and pestle

½ teaspoon coriander seeds, crushed with
   a mortar and pestle

1 bay leaf, coarsely crumbled

20 g / 1 cup fresh dill leaves, chopped

180 g / 1 large beet, grated

680 g / 1½-pound boneless, skin-on salmon fillet

Combine the salt, sugar, spices, and dill in a bowl and stir to combine. Line a sheet pan with plastic wrap and layer a little less than half of the spice mixture on the plastic in a shape that matches the length and width of the salmon fillet. Place the fillet skin-side down on top of the spice mixture and rub the rest of the spice mixture onto the top of the fillet. Cover with an even layer of the grated beet and wrap tightly with plastic, making sure the fillet is lying flat on the sheet pan. Weight the salmon down with another sheet pan and something heavy on top, then place the whole thing in the refrigerator for 3 days. Turn the wrapped fillet over once per day to ensure an even cure, and drain any juices that may accumulate during the curing process.

When the fillet has cured, rinse it under cold water and pat it dry. It will keep wrapped tightly in the refrigerator for up to 1 week before serving.

TRY IT WITH . . . Sliced thinly, this salmon will dazzle your guests when served on a platter with **Crème Fraîche**, **Quickled** shallots or fennel, shaved radishes, and capers. It is excellent paired with **Buttermilk Rye**, **Black Bread**, **Spiced Carrot Levain**, **Miche**, or **Sourdough Whole-Grain Bagels**.

KITCHEN NOTE When elderflowers are in season, I like to substitute 1 cup of the blooms, plucked from their stems, for the beets and dill. This alternative yields a delicate, floral character to the gravlax, so you may wish to use a substantial fillet of a less oily fish such as trout as a substitute for the salmon.

Pickled Shrimp

— MAKES ONE 2-LITER JAR —

Spiked with an exotic mix of spices, these tangy and tender shrimp are easy to make in advance for entertaining or to make your desk lunch a little fancier. If you can't source grains of paradise, curry or lime leaves, or fresh galangal, substitute with coarsely ground black pepper, bay leaves, and fresh ginger, respectively. Green tomatoes that are just beginning to show signs of ripeness are an appropriate addition to this unconventional take on an otherwise Southern staple, but tomatillos, red cherry tomatoes, or a combination are all delicious.

2 whole dried chilies of your choice, halved
   (or more to taste)
1 teaspoon whole coriander seeds
1 teaspoon yellow mustard seeds
½ teaspoon brown mustard seeds
1 teaspoon grains of paradise
1 teaspoon coarsely ground black pepper
215 g / 1 cup extra-virgin olive oil
35 g / 4 to 5 plump garlic cloves, crushed
   and peeled
1-inch piece fresh galangal, thinly sliced
8 whole dried kefir lime leaves

8 whole dried curry leaves
13 g / 2½ teaspoons fine sea salt
225 g / 1 cup white wine vinegar
230 g / 1 cup freshly squeezed lemon juice
905 g / 2 pounds fresh large shrimp, peeled
   and deveined
60 g / 1 lime, thinly sliced
80 g / 1 cup shaved or very thinly sliced
   red onion (about 1 small onion)
80 g / 1 small green tomato, shaved or
   very thinly sliced
2 tablespoons fresh cilantro leaves

In a small skillet, toast the chilies, coriander seeds, mustard seeds, grains of paradise, and pepper over medium-low heat for 2 to 3 minutes or until you hear the mustard seeds just start to pop. Pour in the oil and whisk in the garlic, galangal, kefir lime leaves, curry leaves, and salt and warm for 1 to 2 minutes longer, then remove the skillet from the heat. Stir in the vinegar and lemon juice and set aside to cool.

Prepare an ice bath in a large bowl with 3 cups (680 g) of water and 3 cups (375 g) of ice cubes. Bring 12 cups (2,720 g) of water to boil in a large stock pot. Add the shrimp and allow them to cook for 2 to 3 minutes or until they just begin to curl and turn pink. Using a slotted spoon, transfer the shrimp to the ice bath to halt the cooking process.

In a 2-quart airtight container, pack the lime slices, onion, tomato, cilantro, and cooled shrimp in artfully considered layers, then ladle the marinade and spices in between. Gently press the shrimp mixture with the back of a spoon to submerge it in the liquid, and lightly

tamp the container on the counter to eliminate air bubbles. Store the container in the refrigerator for at least 1 or up to 3 days for the best flavor. Scrape off the whole spices before serving. The shrimp will keep for up to 2 weeks in the refrigerator.

TRY IT WITH . . . These make a simple and flavorful garnish for avocado toast. Nestle some greens on a piece of **Lavash**, layer with cucumbers, pop in a few shrimp, and drizzle with **Tahini Sauce**. Prepare a wonderful chopped salad with these shrimp, a little **Homemade Mayonnaise**, fresh lemon juice, chopped avocado, and fresh corn to serve on a slice of toasted **Pain de Mie**. Smear some **Labneh** or **Crème Fraîche** onto **Garlic Crostini** before topping with a piece of shrimp and some fresh herbs.

Baccalà Mantecato

— MAKES 3¼ CUPS —

The first time I experienced salted fish drying in the sweltering sun was in Livingston, Guatemala. A small port town, which at the time was reachable only by air or water, Livingston lies in steamy isolation at the mouth of the Rio Dulce. The water is murky and the people are a representation of both Mayan ancestry and the striking Garifuna peoples descended from shipwrecked African slaves. The food of Livingston is a lively mix of traditions, but much of the fresh catch of the day is intended for export. Near my open-air guesthouse was a drying facility for salted fish; the odor was unmistakable and the production admirable. Bench after bench was covered in thousands of salted fillets left to dry in the open air, tended to by local fishermen while chickens scurried underfoot and stray cats and dogs languished in the shade. The resulting product is full of minerality and has a shelf life of several years, making it easily transportable.

Salt cod was first introduced to Europe from the Northern Atlantic in the fifteenth century, traded heavily for items such as olive oil. It worked its way into Caribbean cuisine during colonial rule and was considered one of the most important items exchanged between the Old and the New World triangular trading routes. Unfortunately, Atlantic cod has become overfished due to unsustainable bottom trawling; when preparing this recipe, look for Pacific cod that has been trap caught or fished through bottom longlines to ensure that it is sustainably harvested. It has a delicate flavor similar to traditional Atlantic cod and is perfectly suitable for Baccalà Mantecato. You may substitute some of the olive oil with heavy cream, but I prefer this lighter, more versatile version. (Recipe shown on page 158.)

---

455 g / 1 pound salted cod
335 g / 1 large russet potato, peeled and
   boiled until tender
15 g / 2 plump garlic cloves, minced
1 heaping tablespoon finely chopped fresh
   parsley leaves

35 g / 3 tablespoons freshly squeezed
   lemon juice
110 g / ½ cup extra-virgin olive oil
Salt and freshly ground black pepper to taste

Rinse the cod under cold water to remove the salt crystals. Place it in a large bowl and cover with cold water. Cover and soak in the refrigerator for at least 2 days, changing the water once daily.

Remove the cod from the water and cut it into chunks about 4 to 6 inches long, then place them in a large saucepan. Cover with about 2 inches of water and bring to a slow boil over medium-high heat. Cook for 25 to 30 minutes, skimming and discarding any foam that appears on the surface. When the cod begins to easily flake (be careful not to cook it to a mush), use a slotted spoon to transfer it to a large bowl. Add the boiled potato, garlic, parsley, and lemon juice and mash everything together with a fork. Gradually drizzle in the olive oil, a little at a time, mashing well to emulsify the mixture. Season to taste with salt and pepper. (Alternatively, you may perform these steps in a food processor if you prefer a fluffy and smooth texture.) Serve warm or at room temperature, drizzled with more olive oil and garnished with more chopped fresh herbs.

TRY IT WITH . . . This is a perfect appetizer dish or make-ahead lunch sandwich. Grilled **Black Bread**, **Buttermilk Rye**, **Seeded Tahini Pain Rustique**, or even **A Modest Baguette** are perfect for slathering with **Horseradish Apple Cream**, piling high with Baccalà Mantecato, and finishing with **Quickles**, or **Kraut**. Shaved fennel, radishes, beets and/or dill, and a squeeze of lemon will also suffice. As an appetizer, serve this with **Garlic Crostini** and fresh herbs.

You can mix the Baccalà Mantecato with a little cream, top it with grated Parmesan cheese, and bake in a 400°F oven until the cheese is melted and the Baccalà is warmed through, about 15 to 20 minutes.

7

Tartine Toppers

"Learning about food—learning to eat—
is a series of edible adventures and surprises."

—PETER MAYLE, *French Lessons:
Adventures with Knife, Fork, and Corkscrew*

Bread and butter alone are enough to satisfy the simplest needs of mankind, but we are surrounded by endless possibilities for uncomplicated elaboration. When the season fills with alluring produce, the following recipes are reason enough to decadently adorn the table with generous amounts of bread or toast and a quality wine, especially when dining al fresco.

◄ *Top, left to right*: Black Bread, Braised Radicchio in Port Wine, Thyme-Roasted Pears with Red Onion and Gorgonzola. *Bottom, left to right*: Moonbread, Sorghum-Roasted Carrots, Roasted Cherry Tomato Confit, Grilled Escarole.

Spring Medley

— SERVES 6 —

This mélange of spring vegetables marks the break from winter dormancy with a verdant celebration. It is simple to prepare, and you may use a versatile mix of vegetables, substituting at least one-third of the asparagus with fiddleheads and/or morel mushrooms if you can source them. I use shelled peas here, but a combination of shelled peas and halved sugar snap peas would make for a playful presentation.

---

410 g / 1 bunch asparagus, trimmed and cut
  into 4-inch pieces

5 g / 1 teaspoon fine sea salt

1 teaspoon sweet paprika

½ teaspoon freshly ground black pepper

1 teaspoon fresh thyme leaves

15 g / 1 tablespoon unsalted butter

15 g / 1 tablespoon extra-virgin olive oil

50 g / 1 medium shallot, thinly sliced

8 g / 1 plump garlic clove, minced

130 g / 1 cup fresh shelled peas

Generous squeeze fresh lemon juice

1½ tablespoons chopped fresh mint

In a large bowl, toss together the asparagus, salt, paprika, pepper, and thyme; set aside.

In a large, lidded skillet, melt the butter and the olive oil over medium heat. Add the shallot and sauté uncovered until translucent, about 4 to 5 minutes. Stir in the garlic and cook until fragrant, about 30 seconds. Transfer the asparagus to the skillet and stir to combine. Cover the skillet and cook for 8 to 10 minutes or until the asparagus is just fork tender but still quite crisp. Stir in the peas, cover, and continue to cook for 5 more minutes.

Remove the skillet from the heat. Plate the medley, giving a generous squeeze of fresh lemon to finish each serving. Garnish with fresh mint and serve warm or at room temperature.

TRY IT WITH . . . Serve on a split **Spelt English Muffin** with hunks of lobster or smoked salmon, topped with hollandaise. This medley is also delicious served on **Skillet Toast** of your choosing, drizzled with **Tahini Sauce** and/or smeared with **Ramp and Carrot Top Pesto Spread**. As an alternative, use a little **Lemony Herb Chèvre** on **Dry Toast** or **Garlic Crostini** before heaping on a generous serving of these warm vegetables.

Sorghum-Roasted Carrots

— SERVES 4 TO 6 —

My favorite time to prepare this warming dish is in early winter or late spring, when green-market carrots have had ample time in the cold ground to concentrate their sugars and turn naturally sweet. Sorghum syrup is a typically Southern ingredient, similar to molasses but lighter and fruitier in flavor. If you can source bourbon barrel–aged sorghum, you will have a very special addition that will leave your guests wondering what your secret ingredient is! If you cannot source sorghum of any kind, substitute with ½ tablespoon of molasses and 1 tablespoon of mild honey. If you can source baby carrots, they make for a special, succulent dish that will require less time to roast. (Recipe shown on page 220.)

455 g / 1 pound carrots, quartered lengthwise if
    large and cut into 4-inch pieces
30 g / 2 tablespoons extra-virgin olive oil
30 g / 1½ tablespoons sorghum syrup
½ teaspoon whole cumin seeds
½ teaspoon ground coriander or several heads
    fresh green coriander
8 g / 1½ teaspoons Harissa, or to taste
    (page 177)
5 g / 1 teaspoon fine sea salt
15 g / 1 tablespoon unsalted butter, melted
Generous squeeze fresh lemon juice

FOR THE GARNISH
2 tablespoons S'chug (page 175) or Ramp and
    Carrot Top Pesto Spread (page 173)
or
1½ tablespoons chopped fresh cilantro
    and/or mint

Preheat your oven to 425°F. In a large bowl, toss together the carrots, oil, sorghum syrup, spices, and salt. Spread the mixture evenly on a large sheet pan, being careful not to crowd the carrots. Roast for about 20 minutes, stirring occasionally, until the carrots are caramelized and tender but still slightly crunchy. Remove them from the oven, drizzle with the melted butter, and add a squeeze of fresh lemon to finish.

    Plate and garnish with S'chug, Ramp and Carrot Top Pesto Spread, or cilantro and/or mint and serve warm or at room temperature.

TRY IT WITH . . . These sweet and spicy carrots are delightful drizzled with **Tahini Sauce**, served on **Dry Toast** spread with **Ramp and Carrot Top Pesto Spread**, or sprinkled generously with **S'chug**. **Spiced Carrot Levain** is an appropriate foil for this dish, but **Black Bread**, **Buttermilk Rye**, **Miche**, and **Seeded Tahini Pain Rustique** are all equally delicious.

KITCHEN NOTE If you wish for your carrots to have a slightly smoky char to them, once the carrots have roasted for about 15 minutes, set the oven to broil and place the sheet pan directly under the broiler for about 2 to 3 minutes, depending on your oven. Watch closely and remove the carrots from the oven when they are slightly charred.

Pan-Fried Cauliflower in Curried Yogurt Marinade

— SERVES 8 TO 10 —

Yogurt is not only a delicious marinade, but also an excellent tenderizer. The lactic acid bacteria naturally present in yogurt work to break down the sometimes tough textures of meats and are equally effective with cauliflower. This creamy, golden dish is delicious served straight from the skillet, and it's even better reheated the next day.

730 g / 1 large head cauliflower

100 g / 2 shallots, thinly sliced

25 g / 3 plump garlic cloves, minced

225 g / 1 cup whole-milk yogurt

15 g / 3 teaspoons Harissa, to taste

25 g / 1½ tablespoons finely diced Preserved Lemons (page 189), rinsed

8 g / 1½ teaspoons fine sea salt

1 heaping teaspoon grated fresh ginger

½ teaspoon crushed dried curry or kefir lime leaves

½ teaspoon ground turmeric

50 g / ¼ cup coconut oil

Remove the outer leaves of the cauliflower and separate the head into the largest sections, leaving the stems intact. Cut each piece into ½-inch-thick slices, allowing the florets to crumble as they will. Transfer the sliced cauliflower to a large bowl and toss it with the shallots and garlic.

In a separate small bowl, whisk together the yogurt, harissa, preserved lemon, salt, and spices. Pour the yogurt mixture over the cauliflower mixture and gently stir to combine. Cover and allow to marinate at room temperature for at least 30 minutes, or refrigerate for up to 24 hours.

Heat half of the oil in a large, heavy-bottomed skillet over medium heat until clear and barely smoking, about 3 minutes. Turn about half of the cauliflower mixture into the skillet, spreading it out to prevent crowding. Cover the skillet and cook for about 15 minutes. Remove the lid and continue cooking until the cauliflower is nicely browned and the yogurt sauce has completely reduced. The cauliflower should be fork tender but not soft. Remove the cooked cauliflower with a slotted spoon and keep it covered in a warm location. Scrape any remaining bits from the pan before adding the remaining oil. Repeat the cooking process with the remaining cauliflower mixture.

TRY IT WITH . . . One of my favorite lunches is a large piece of **Lavash** slathered with **Preserved Lemon and Fava Bean Hummus** and topped with this cauliflower, roasted red peppers, whole-milk yogurt, chopped fresh herbs, and a generous sprinkling of **Dukkah**.

Roasted Cherry Tomato Confit

— MAKES ABOUT 2 CUPS (400 G) —

Roasting vegetables or fruit only intensifies their flavor, and this recipe is no exception. Serve it with toast that has been smeared with generous dollops of fresh Ricotta (page 211) if you want a more robust serving, or simply grate a little Parmesan over the top for an easy finish. This is also a wonderful candidate for tossing with fresh pasta.

110 g / ½ cup extra-virgin olive oil

30 g / 5 plump garlic cloves, crushed and peeled

550 g / 4 cups cherry tomatoes

10 g / 1 tablespoon balsamic vinegar

A few large sprigs thyme and/or rosemary

½ teaspoon fine sea salt

½ teaspoon red pepper flakes

FOR THE GARNISH (OPTIONAL)

1 small handful fresh herbs, chopped

1 to 2 tablespoons freshly grated
    Parmesan cheese

Pinch of flaked sea salt

Preheat your oven to 450°F. Place the oil and garlic in an ovenproof skillet or roasting pan and roast for 8 to 10 minutes or until the garlic is tender and beginning to turn golden, being careful not to let it burn. Remove from the oven and set aside.

Add the tomatoes, balsamic vinegar, herb sprigs, salt, and red pepper flakes to the pan and toss to coat. Return the pan to the oven and roast for 15 to 20 minutes or until the tomatoes are plump and bursting and the skins are blistered and beginning to caramelize. Serve warm or at room temperature, sprinkled with fresh herbs, grated Parmesan, and flaked sea salt.

TRY IT WITH . . . Spoon over **Moonbread**, **Miche**, **A Modest Baguette**, or **Seeded Tahini Pain Rustique**, making sure to sop up the aromatic olive oil with extra bread served on the side! This dish is also excellent served with the freshest Burrata cheese you can source.

Braised Radicchio in Port Wine

— MAKES ABOUT 1 CUP —

Radicchio is a type of bitter chicory that has deep roots in Northern Italy. The most commonly grown cultivar in the United States is the tightly rounded heads of Radicchio di Chioggia, which can be found in most grocery stores. Its tender, deep burgundy leaves with striking white veins are a result of a labor-intensive cultivation process. Other highly decorative varieties—such as Treviso, with its elongated heads of elegantly torqued leaves—are beginning to appear in North America by way of specialty growers and small-scale farmers. It is an excellent cold-weather vegetable crop that can be used in small amounts to add flavor to salads, or braised to mellow its bitter flavor. Double or triple this recipe to feed a large crowd. (Recipe shown on page 220.)

About 275 g / 1 head radicchio

30 g / 2 tablespoons extra-virgin olive oil

3 g / ½ teaspoon fine sea salt

60 g / ½ cup thinly sliced red onion

1 small sprig rosemary

55 g / ¼ cup port wine

10 g / 1 tablespoon balsamic vinegar

Generous squeeze fresh lemon juice

FOR THE GARNISH (OPTIONAL)

1½ tablespoons coarsely chopped pine nuts
 or hazelnuts

45 g / ⅓ cup crumbled blue cheese

Chopped fresh herbs, such as parsley or chives

Cut the radicchio into quarters if using an elongated variety, or into eighths if using a rounder variety. (If the root ends are still attached, trim them off but do not core the head. This will encourage the pieces to stay intact while cooking.) Place the oil in a heavy-bottomed skillet with a lid and roll to coat the bottom of the pan. Place the skillet over medium heat and warm until the oil is clear and just beginning to smoke. Carefully place the radicchio pieces in the skillet, sprinkle with the salt, and allow them to brown for 2 to 3 minutes. Using tongs, turn the pieces over and brown them for another 2 to 3 minutes on the other side.

Sprinkle the onions in between the browned radicchio pieces and nestle the rosemary into the pan. Pour in the port wine and vinegar, cover the skillet, and reduce the heat to low. Cook for about 15 minutes or until the radicchio is almost tender. Remove the lid and continue cooking until the mixture appears caramelized and the liquid has evaporated, another

5 to 6 minutes. Transfer the mixture to a warm serving dish and garnish with pine nuts, blue cheese, and herbs (if using). Serve warm.

TRY IT WITH . . . This dish is excellent served with **Miche**, **Buttermilk Rye**, **Black Bread**, **Seeded Tahini Pain Rustique**, or **Spiced Carrot Levain**, **Dry Toasted** and daubed with **Labneh**.

Thyme-Roasted Pears with Red Onion & Gorgonzola

— SERVES 4 TO 6 —

This woodsy, autumn dish is made noteworthy by a drizzling of Infused Honey (page 149). Either the Smoky Cardamom, Juniper, and Anise Seed or the Vanilla Orange Spice variation plays beautifully with the sweetness of the pears and the savory saltiness of the gorgonzola. (Recipe shown on page 221.)

---

440 g / 2 large pears, cored and cut into
    ¼-inch-thick slices

60 g / 1 small red onion, cut into
    ¼-inch-thick slices

½ tablespoon fresh thyme leaves

¼ teaspoon ground nutmeg

¼ teaspoon Citrus Salt (page 183)

¼ teaspoon freshly ground black pepper

40 g / 2½ tablespoons extra-virgin
    olive oil

5 g / 1 teaspoon apple cider vinegar

70 g / ½ cup crumbled gorgonzola cheese

FOR THE GARNISH

40 to 60 g / 2 to 3 tablespoons Infused Honey
    (page 149)

Preheat your oven to 400°F. In a small baking dish, toss together the pears, onion, thyme, nutmeg, Citrus Salt, pepper, olive oil, and the vinegar. Roast for about 15 to 20 minutes, until the onions soften, then remove the dish from the oven. Immediately sprinkle the gorgonzola over the top, drizzle with the honey, and serve.

TRY IT WITH . . . This dish pairs nicely with pan-wilted bitter greens, such as dandelion or chicory, on a seasonal tartine. Simply heat 1½ tablespoons of oil or bacon fat in a pan and toss in 2 generous handfuls of thoroughly cleaned, roughly chopped leaves. Season lightly with salt and cook until wilted and deep, vibrant green in color, about 7 minutes. Arrange on buttered **Skillet Toast** and dress with the roasted pears, cheese, and honey on top. Serve warm drizzled with **Infused Honey**.

Grilled Escarole

— SERVES 4 —

Escarole is a slightly bitter green that turns buttery and almost smoky-sweet when grilled. Belonging to the chicory family, it looks much like a head of leafy romaine lettuce, although it is a decidedly beefier cool-season green. Look for it in specialty food stores or ask your favorite farmer. If you do not have access to a grill, heat the oil in a skillet over high heat and sear the escarole cut-side down, flipping and cooking until tender.

About 600 g / 4 large heads escarole, washed

30 to 45 g / 2 to 3 tablespoons extra-virgin
olive oil

1 teaspoon Citrus Salt (page 183)

Freshly ground black pepper, to taste

FOR THE GARNISH

125 g / ½ cup savory Tahini Sauce (page 157)

1 tablespoon Dukkah (page 184)

Generous squeeze fresh lemon juice

Lightly oil the grate of an outdoor grill and preheat to medium high. Cut the heads of the escarole in half lengthwise and brush the cut sides liberally with olive oil. (Alternatively, if the heads are small, leave them intact.) Sprinkle the cut sides with the Citrus Salt and some black pepper, then flip them over and lightly brush the outside leaves with oil. Place the escarole halves on the grill, cut-sides down, and grill them until the leaves begin to wilt and brown, about 3 to 5 minutes. Serve warm, topped with the Tahini Sauce, Dukkah, and lemon juice.

TRY IT WITH . . . This beautiful grilled vegetable is delicious served atop **Lavash** or on **Garlic Crostini** made with **A Modest Baguette**, wedges of **Moonbread**, **Black Bread**, or any hearth loaf of your choosing.

Warm Brussels Sprouts Salad

— MAKES ABOUT 3½ CUPS —

Brussels sprouts and preserved lemon combine in a mutually flattering composition in this easily assembled, warm skillet salad. Enoki mushrooms grant a playful texture that cooks up quickly, but you can substitute them with oyster mushrooms or a meatier, impressive trumpet, finely diced.

8 g / ½ tablespoon unsalted butter

8 g / ½ tablespoon extra-virgin olive oil

60 g / ½ cup thinly sliced red onion

15 g / 2 plump garlic cloves, minced

100 g / 1 heaping cup torn enoki mushrooms

340 g / 2¾ cups shaved Brussels sprouts

1 teaspoon Citrus Salt or Herb Salt
(pages 183 and 182)

45 g / 3 tablespoons diced Preserved Lemons
(page 189), rinsed

Melt the butter and olive oil in a heavy-bottomed skillet over medium heat. Add the onions and sauté until translucent, about 7 to 8 minutes. Stir in the garlic and continue to cook for about 30 seconds or until fragrant. Toss the enokis with the onion-garlic mixture and sauté until the mushrooms begin to release their juices, about 5 minutes. Add the shaved Brussels sprouts, sprinkle in the salt, and cook just until the Brussels sprouts are tender, another 6 to 7 minutes. Turn off the heat and fold the preserved lemon into the mixture. Serve warm or at room temperature.

TRY IT WITH . . . This is an excellent brunch item served over **Spelt English Muffins**, **Moonbread**, **Black Bread**, **Miche**, or **Spiced Carrot Levain** and drizzled with **Tahini Sauce**. Of course, if you put an egg on it, that wouldn't hurt either.